LEADING OUT-OF-THE-BOX CHANGE

The Chief Executive's
Essential Guide to
Achieving Nonprofit
Innovation and Growth

By
Doug Eadie
President & CEO
Doug Eadie & Company, Inc.

A Governance Edge® Publication

A publication of
Governance Edge®
Doug Eadie & Company
3 Sunny Point Terrace
Oldsmar, FL 34677

Phone: 800.209.7652
Email: info@GovernanceEdge.com
A complete listing of books and CDs by Doug Eadie is available at www.DougEadie.com.

Copyright © 2012 by Doug Eadie & Company. All rights reserved. No part of this publication may be reproduced, stored, distributed, or transmitted in any form or by any means, electronic or mechanical, except in the case of brief quotations embodied in critical reviews and certain other noncommercial uses permitted by copyright law, without prior written permission from Doug Eadie & Company. Please direct requests to the address shown above.

ISBN 978-0-9798894-8-6

Library of Congress Control Number: 2011945074

Library of Congress Subject Headings:
Organizational change-Management
Nonprofit organizations-Management

For my wife, Barbara, and our children,
Donna, Jennifer, Kevin, Sean, Steve, and William

TABLE OF CONTENTS

Foreword   vii

Acknowledgments   ix

Overview
Out-of-the-Box Change in a Nutshell   1

Chapter One
Powerful and Passionate CEO Leadership   9

Chapter Two
Out-of-the-Box Change Planning
and Management   35

Chapter Three
Intensive Governing Body Involvement   65

Postscript
Up Close and Personal   89

FOREWORD

What a great time to be a leader! These are exciting, high-opportunity times for nonprofit and public organizations. The rapid — and rapidly accelerating — change that's swirling around our organizations these days, while it can be a bit bewildering, sends myriad opportunities our way to come up with innovative new products, programs, and services to meet new needs and demands from our customers, clients and members. However, the rapid change that characterizes today's world is a mixed blessing, as you well know. Along with opportunities galore come challenges and threats aplenty. This is definitely not the ideal world for the slow-moving, fainthearted or risk-averse leader.

I'm sure you'll agree with me that the nonprofit and public organizations that are smart, aggressive and nimble enough to take command of their own change — rather than merely being changed by the forces swirling around them — will be the ones that succeed, thriving and growing over the long run. So Doug Eadie's *Leading Out-of-the-Box Change* has come along at just the right time. Doug's power-packed little book is filled with very practical, concrete wisdom that you can put to immediate use in your organization — whatever its mission, size, and circumstances — to grapple with the highest stakes, most complex opportunities and challenges — in Doug's words, the "out-of-the-box" issues — your organization is facing.

What makes Doug's book a particularly rich resource for nonprofit and public leaders is its grounding in Doug's quarter century of hands-on work with an incredible range of organizations. *Leading Out-of-the-Box Change* is a real-life guidebook, for real-life leaders who are facing real-life challenges — not just another one of those collections of fascinating but untested theories. The beauty of the Change Investment Portfolio Process that Doug describes in this book isn't that it's exotic, theoretically speaking, but that it actually works as a powerful out-of-the-box change tool.

I'm delighted to recommend this book to you, and I know that you'll want to make it a valued addition to the small collection of truly precious resources on your leadership bookshelf.

Christie A. Tarantino, CAE
President & CEO
Association Forum of Chicagoland

ACKNOWLEDGMENTS

The practical wisdom that I share in this book is based on my work with the board members, chief executives, and senior managers of over 500 nonprofit and public organizations. I am fortunate to have worked with so many dedicated leaders doing such important work in so many fields. I owe them a debt of gratitude for enriching my professional life and teaching me what I needed to know to write *Leading Out-of-the-Box Change*.

Several outstanding leaders reviewed portions of the manuscript of this book, and their insightful comments have helped to make *Leading Out-of-the-Box Change* a more powerful resource for nonprofit and public sector practitioners. My thanks to: Abe Abraham, President/CEO, CMI Management, Inc.; Michael Allegra, General Manager, Utah Transit Authority; Carm Basile, Chief Executive Officer, Capital District Transportation Authority; Steve Bland, Chief Executive Officer, Port Authority of Allegheny County; David Boggs, Executive Director, Regional Public Transportation Authority (Phoenix, Arizona); Pamela Boswell, Vice President, Program Management/Educational Services, American Public Transportation Association; Ronnie Bryant, President & CEO, Charlotte Regional Partnership; Sue Buchholtz, President/CEO, Evergreen Presbyterian Ministries; Norman Dolch, Editor-in-Chief, *Journal of Nonprofit Education and Leadership*, and Professor, University of North Texas; Maling Ebrahimpour, Dean and Professor, College of Business, University of South Florida - St. Petersburg; Melissa Fahy, Executive Director, Good Samaritan Health Clinic of Pasco County; Jeff Finkle, President & CEO, International Economic Development Council; Kurt Foreman, President, North Louisiana Economic Partnership; Christopher Fox, Executive Director, International Association for Dental Research; Tim Groshens, Executive Director, Minnesota State Bar Association; J.R. Harding, External Affairs Manager, Florida Agency for Persons with Disabilities; Virginia Jacko, President & CEO, Miami Lighthouse for the Blind and Visually Impaired; Linda Kloss, CEO, Kloss Strategic Advisers, Ltd.; Joan Lamson, Board Member, Leadership North Carolina; Gregory Maciag, President & CEO, ACORD; James McGuirk, Executive Director/CEO, Astor Services for Children and Families; Gene Marshall, Chair of the Board of Trustees, Community Foundation of Tampa Bay; Susan Meyer, Chief Executive Officer, Spokane Transit Authority; Elinor Paladine, Vice Chair of the Board of Directors, Good Samaritan Health Clinic of Pasco County; Cheryl Ronk, President/CEO, Michigan Society of Association Executives; Brent Routman, President, Minnesota State Bar Association; David Schmidt, General Secretary, Beta Theta Pi; David Stackrow, Past Chair and member of the Board of Directors, Capital District Transportation Authority; Christie Tarantino, President & CEO, Association Forum of Chicagoland; Gary Thomas, President, American Public Transportation Association and President/Executive Director, Dallas Area Rapid Transit; Jim Thompson, Executive Director, Association Executives of North Carolina; Lana Vukovljak, Chief Executive Officer, American Association of Diabetes Educators; and Tesfagiorgis Wondimagegnehu, formerly Head of the Planning, Policy Analysis and Review Department of the Ethiopian Civil Service Commission.

Tom Berger, CEO of Orange Street Editorial and my longtime friend and colleague, did his typically very capable job of editing the manuscript of *Leading Out-of-the-Box Change* and shepherding it through the production process. Tracey Burns and Misty Kirn on the Doug Eadie & Company team provided me with the administrative support that allowed me to concentrate on my writing task rather than worrying about day-to-day operations.

My children, Jennifer and William, who both held senior positions in the nonprofit and public sectors before launching their careers in the law, provided not only strong encouragement, but also very practical and insightful counsel as I worked on this book. And Kay Sue Nagle, my sister and dear friend, drew on her wide-ranging professional and volunteer experience in making a number of very useful recommendations for improving the manuscript.

Last, but far from least, Barbara Krai, my wife and closest friend, once again — as she has so many times before — took time from her highly successful and demanding interior design business to make this a far better book than it otherwise would have been. Not only did Barbara bring her keen artist's eye to the cover design, she also drew on years of high-level nonprofit volunteering — including membership on the Women's Council of the wonderful Cleveland Museum of Art and on the board of the Women's City Club of Cleveland — to refine several of the key concepts in this book. And, of course, her unconditional love and companionship were a source of tremendous strength as I juggled the writing task with my work as a speaker and consultant. As always, I am in her debt.

Doug Eadie
Oldsmar, Florida

Overview

OUT-OF-THE-BOX CHANGE IN A NUTSHELL

NO WAY OF AVOIDING CHANGE

In today's and tomorrow's rapidly changing, always challenging world, neither you, as an individual, nor your organization is free to choose the no-change option. You really have only one choice: You can take the initiative and manage your own change, or you can just let yourself be changed by forces in the world around you. There's no middle ground, no hope of hunkering down and standing pat. The price of inaction — of sitting back and letting change happen to you — can be pretty steep. You can fail to capitalize on important growth opportunities (for example, missing out on a major grant to fund planning a new light rail service; failing to forge an alliance with a hospital that is a key potential partner). You can also incur some painful direct costs (for example, having to lay off staff because you didn't get a firm handle on costs; losing members because you didn't make an effort to update your association's educational services for its rapidly changing membership; abysmal test scores in one of your schools because you've neglected staff development).

STAYING IN THE BOX

But even when individuals and organizations do become active participants in the change game, more often than not, in my experience, they tend to play it safe by focusing almost exclusively on what I call "in-the-box" change, which involves incrementally tweaking existing programs, services and functions. In-the-box change is a mainstream process that's carried out within the boundaries of your organization's current mission (a snapshot of what you're all about, in terms of programs and services, clients and customers, and how you go about serving your clients and customers). And your annual operational planning and budget development process is your most reliable mainstream tool for generating such in-the-box change. Here are some real-life examples of in-the-box-change: trimming back on certain costs because of reductions in state funding; updating a training program for your bus drivers on interacting with riders; creating a new position of assistant development director to beef up your fundraising; diversifying your annual conference sessions to attract more registrants; acquiring new computer equipment for your language lab; and fine-tuning your manual of governance policies and procedures.

I don't want you to feel guilty about paying lots of attention to ongoing, mainstream change that fits quite nicely in the box. While it may be familiar, comfortable, usually unexciting and often uninspiring, incremental change that's in the box is one of the keys to your organization's success. It's your preeminent continuous improvement tool, through which you enhance your organization's effectiveness and efficiency and maintain the stability that breeds confidence and commitment among staff, board members, and key external stakeholders. Therefore, it makes the best of sense for you to pay close attention to your organization's annual operational planning and budget-preparation process, making sure that it's consciously designed to fine-tune your organization's current programs, services, and functions — inside the box. That's why many of my clients have built into their annual planning process intensive front-end board and executive team involvement in identifying operational improvement issues that need to be addressed in putting together the annual plan and budget.

BUT IF YOU WANT TO THRIVE AND GROW

Continuously tweaking and strengthening your nonprofit or public organization's programs, services and functions will pay off handsomely — no question — but what it won't do is ensure that your organization thrives and grows over the long haul in our rapidly changing, always-challenging world. That's why I wrote *Leading Out-of-the-Box Change*. What do I mean by "out-of-the-box" change? In a nutshell, out-of-the-box change:

- **Is driven by your organization's vision** (beyond the boundaries of your mission!), in terms of what it aspires to be and to do over the long run: the range of services and products you envision offering; the mix of clients and customers you envision serving; and the organizational structure you envision creating (for example, do you see yourself growing by actively pursuing mergers and/or acquisitions?).

- **Is explicitly focused on generating significant innovation** that transcends programmatic and functional boundaries in order to grow your organization within the framework of your vision for the future.

- **Focuses on out-of-the-box issues** — in the form of opportunities to grow and challenges and threats standing in the way of growth — that cannot be effectively handled by the annual operational planning/budget preparation process because of their technical and/or political complexity and the amount of risk involved.

- **Tends to make a much larger claim on resources** — primarily time, money, and political capital — than in-the-box incremental change because of the focus on significant innovation, and also tends to be much more difficult to manage than more incremental change.
- **And depends heavily on creative input** (which I define as your organization's capacity to generate possibilities for change — as your preeminent source of newness).

Examples of out-of-the-box change that clients of mine have accomplished include a public transportation agency building a light rail line to supplement its traditional bus service; a community college creating a stand-alone high-tech training center separate from its three campuses in partnership with local corporations; a school district completely revamping the process of evaluating teacher effectiveness with the aid of a handsome foundation grant; a nursing home diversifying into assisted living as part of its vision to encompass the whole continuum of care; a social service agency expanding and restructuring its governing board in the interest of stronger strategic decision making; and an international association consummating a complex, high-stakes merger with a sister association in the same industry. When you think about it, you can see that not one of these significant change initiatives could have been handled through the business-as-usual operational planning and budgeting process. They don't fit in any of the conventional operational boxes; in short, they're out-of-the-box changes.

THE ROAD LESS TRAVELED

I learned very early in my career — back in Cleveland, Ohio, when I was working as a middle manager at the Council for Economic Opportunities — that really significant, self-planned and self-managed change of the out-of-the-box variety is not only extraordinarily difficult to accomplish, it's also the distinct exception to the rule. Why don't more individuals and their organizations take hold of the change reins and take command of their own out-of-the-box change? Five closely related barriers loom largest, in my experience:

- The chief executive officer does not play a highly visible, aggressive leadership role in leading out-of-the-box change, so there's not enough top-down guidance, direction, support, and pressure to keep the out-of-the-box change process moving ahead.

- At the technical end of the spectrum, the mechanics of a well-designed planning process that is dedicated to generating out-of-the-box change initiatives haven't been worked out and firmly established.

- The governing body (board, commission, or council) does not function as a powerful champion for change initiatives due to inadequate involvement in out-of-the-box change planning.

- At the emotional/psychological end of the spectrum, not enough attention has been paid to overcoming the normal human resistance to changing in important ways.

- And then there's always the *now* that threatens to overwhelm significant change. Time and resources are all-too-scarce, and the pressures and distractions of day-to-day operations can feel overwhelming.

BEATING THE ODDS

I wrote *Leading Out-of-the-Box Change* to arm you with very detailed, practical, down-to-earth guidance that you can put to immediate use — in your nonprofit or public organization and even in your personal life — in beating the odds and accomplishing significant out-of-the-box change. The guidance that I share in the following pages draws on contemporary planning and management theory, but I don't waste your time by merely summarizing what other authors have written on the subject of change. Rather, all of the advice and counsel in this very practical guidebook is based on my work as a senior executive in the nonprofit and public sectors and as a consultant to over 500 nonprofit and public organizations.

Accomplishing significant change and building solid board-chief executive partnerships have been my twin professional foci and passions for over twenty-five years, and the wisdom I share in this guidebook has been thoroughly tested through my work with the governing bodies, chief executives, and senior executives of international and national associations, economic and community development corporations, public school districts, postsecondary educational institutions, providers of health care, aging and social services organizations, and public transportation authorities. Of course, changing in major ways always involves some risk and hence requires a good dollop of courage, but the advice and counsel in this guidebook will help you keep the risk within reasonable bounds.

Leading Out-of-the-Box Change consists of three main chapters and a Postscript:

Chapter One: Powerful and Passionate CEO Leadership

Every successful out-of-the-box change process I've observed has been led from the top down — by the organization's chief executive officer, serving as the organization's Innovator-in-Chief. Working closely with her governing body, the change-savvy CEO wears three hats as Innovator-in-Chief: Chief Process Designer, Chief Motivator, and Chief Enabler.

Chapter Two: Out-of-the-Box Change Planning and Management

This chapter describes the Change Investment Portfolio Process, a powerful, thoroughly tested approach for accomplishing out-of-the-box change. The Portfolio Process involves: identifying and analyzing out-of-the-box issues in the form of opportunities for growth and challenges facing your organization; selecting the issues on which your organization should focus now; and fashioning and implementing change initiatives to address the selected issues. Successfully accomplishing out-of-the-box change also depends on a dedicated management structure that is separate from the structure for managing day-to-day operations.

Chapter Three: Intensive Governing Body Involvement

The governing body — whether a board of directors or trustees, a city council, or county commission — must be your organization's preeminent "change champion" if you are to accomplish out-of-the-box change. Only your governing body has the authority to adopt plans and strategies and to commit financial resources to implementing out-of-the-box change initiatives. Also, strong, consistent board backing for your chief executive officer is critical to countering the normal human resistance to change and, consequently, getting initiatives implemented.

Postscript: Up Close and Personal

Building the capacity to lead out-of-the-box change is not only critical to organizational success in a changing, challenging world, but it is also the key to individuals' leading fuller and more satisfying personal and professional lives. The principles and techniques discussed in Chapters One, Two, and Three can, with appropriate tailoring, be applied by individuals in planning and managing their own growth and development.

A PASSIONATE ENDEAVOR

Writing *Leading Out-of-the-Box Change* has been a passionate endeavor for me for two reasons. First, over the years I have been appalled at the cost to individuals and organizations of failing to lead and manage significant change effectively — in terms of underserved clients, unmet needs, fiscal crises, unfulfilled visions and thwarted human potential, dashed dreams, and half-lived lives. Second, I have personally learned in my own life and career how important taking command of change is to living fuller, more satisfying and productive personal and professional lives. I would never hold myself up, however, as a paragon of orderly, painless change. Rather, I am but a fellow sufferer on the road less traveled, who has had fears aplenty to contend with in my own journey, and I'm sure there'll be new ones down the road to face. I trust that my own often painful struggles to change in many ways over the years have made me a wiser and more empathic counselor, but you, the reader, will be the judge of that.

Chapter One

POWERFUL AND PASSIONATE CEO LEADERSHIP

THE INNOVATOR-IN-CHIEF

I've earned a good deal of my daily bread over the past quarter century helping nonprofit and public organizations plan and implement out-of-the-box change, and I've gotten pretty good at quickly calculating the odds that a particular organization will be able to get significant change accomplished. The surest sign of likely success in the out-of-the-box change game, in my experience, is a chief executive officer (CEO) who is passionately committed to playing — and well prepared to play — what I call the "Innovator-in-Chief" role. CEOs who excel at the Innovator-in-Chief role first and foremost make accomplishing out-of-the-box change a top-tier chief executive leadership priority. They also bring to the out-of-the-box change game substantial technical planning know-how, strong psychological and political skills, a large dollop of discipline and courage, and the internal stature to lead the change charge.

I was fortunate to learn early in my career as a change consultant that successful out-of-the-box change hinges on extraordinary CEO leadership, and it's served me well over the years. It's certainly kept me from getting embroiled in Don Quixote-like change efforts that are highly likely to crash and burn, jeopardizing my professional reputation. Believe me, whenever I come across a CEO lacking the rock-solid commitment, know-how, and wherewithal to lead out-of-the-box change, I steer clear of involvement because the deck's too heavily stacked against success for me to get involved.

The CEO is the only person in your organization who can wear the Innovator-in-Chief hat for the simple reason that no one else brings to the change game the formal authority, influence, access to resources, and time required to spearhead an out-of-the-box change effort and to overcome the inevitable inertia and resistance that can sink a change ship early in its voyage. Don't get me wrong; I'm not saying that out-of-the-box change is just a top-down process or that your CEO could get the change job done on his own. Of course not! Without the backing of his board your CEO couldn't possibly succeed in the Innovator-in-Chief role. And it's obvious that the bulk of the nuts-and-bolts work of planning and developing out-of-the-box change initiatives must be done by staff and volunteers. But the fact remains: Without a committed, capable Innovator-in-Chief ensconced in the chief executive suite, out-of-the-box change will almost certainly be the impossible dream.

A ROSE BY ANY OTHER NAME

Before exploring what's involved in your CEO's leading out-of-the-box change, I'd like to say a word about the chief executive officer position in nonprofit and public organizations. It's universally defined as the highest ranking, almost always full-time, paid professional staff member who is hired by, and reports directly to, the governing body, is responsible for all internal operations, and — typically along with your board chair — is the public face of your organization. The man or woman holding the chief executive reins goes by a variety of titles in different organizations, such as *chief executive officer*, *CEO*, *president*, *president & CEO*, *mayor*, *city manager*, *general manager* (of a public transportation authority), *superintendent* (of a school system), *executive director* and even occasionally *executive vice president* in certain associations. The title *president* sometimes refers to the chair of an organization's governing body, who is the top volunteer and definitely not the chief executive. Also keep in mind that the titles *chief operating officer* and *chief administrative officer* typically refer to second-tier positions reporting to the chief executive officer. For convenience, I will use the title *CEO* from this point on to refer to the chief executive officer of any public or nonprofit organization.

THE CHANGE-SAVVY INNOVATOR-IN-CHIEF

CEOs who succeed in the Innovator-in-Chief role are what I think of as change-savvy. The change-savvy CEOs that I've worked with and observed:

- Are technically very knowledgeable about best practices in the rapidly changing area of change planning and management, which means she isn't wedded to conventional planning wisdom and out-of-date approaches. You'll never hear a change-savvy CEO extolling the virtues of traditional long-range (or strategic) planning as a change tool, much less catch her fondling a ten-pound five-year plan.

- Realize that successfully bringing off out-of-the-box change against all odds requires that she make leading the change planning and implementation process a top-tier priority. In practice, this means that the change-savvy CEO makes a firm commitment of time to leading change from the top and never tries to delegate one piece or another of this leadership role to lieutenants.

- Recognize that leading out-of-the-box change as Innovator-in-Chief of the organization is more psychological and political in nature than technical. Not only does the change-savvy CEO understand that fear is more often than not at the heart of staff resistance to change, she also takes strong, visible steps to allay that fear through the clear articulation of vision and other motivational steps that are intended to inspire and energize participants in the change process. The change-savvy CEO also pays close attention to the transformation of key stakeholders into ardent change champions.

- And command the respect of staff members and key stakeholders, primarily by playing a very aggressive and visible change-leadership role and practicing what she's preaching in the change arena. A change-savvy CEO knows that her leadership credibility depends on walking the talk, never contradicting in practice what she's saying publicly.

In addition to the characteristics I've just described, the CEOs I've observed who have been most successful at accomplishing out-of-the box change have possessed three powerful character traits: courage; deep emotional self-awareness; and fundamental self-confidence. Being courageous and steadfast in leading change planning and management is a critical CEO trait. It never fails: The farther change planning moves outside the box in your organization, the more fear, anxiety, tension, and often anger you're likely to see. As you've probably observed, fear (which feels quite weak) is often quickly transformed into indignation (which feels far stronger), and who's a more convenient culprit and target of anger than the highly visible Innovator-in-Chief who's leading the change charge? The CEOs I've seen do a great job of leading out-of-the-box change are loaded with calcium. That doesn't mean they're insensitive Genghis Khans bludgeoning staff into change — quite the contrary. But it does mean they don't cave under pressure. They expect the resistance and frequent anger, and they withstand it.

The absence of deep emotional self-awareness can seriously limit the impact of a CEO in leading out-of-the-box change. I've seen CEOs who couldn't capitalize on the talents and commitment of strong women on their executive teams because they found such strengths threatening. I've observed CEOs who were unsuccessful in building critical partnerships and joint ventures with other organizations because they saw the world as a dark and dangerous place filled with competitors waiting to do them in. And I've come across CEOs whose need for security and control made them intolerant of the give-and-take of wide-open discussion and led them to impose on their organizations mechanistic long-range planning processes that substituted neatness and order for creative questioning and exploration. In these and other cases, what has struck me over the years is how hidden, unrecognized emotions can sabotage CEOs, causing them to see the world through an internal lens that distorts objective reality, and, hence, leads to inappropriate behavior.

I know that this might sound like psychobabble to some readers, but long experience has convinced me that the most effective change leaders are emotionally so self-knowledgeable that they aren't easily sabotaged by deep-seated emotions they aren't aware of. A few years ago, I worked with just such a CEO, who headed a large and highly successful senior services nonprofit. We were chatting one evening after getting through the first day of an intensive 1 ½-day work session kicking off the organization's change planning process, when she confided that at one point in what'd been a great day she'd felt like lashing out at two of her board members. She said that when they'd raised some pretty pointed questions about her decision to pursue a merger with a sister agency a couple of months earlier, she out of the blue felt like a little girl again, being harshly judged by her parents, and the sudden surge of anger caught her off guard. Fortunately, she didn't lash out, knowing that the anger — while a real emotion that she'd truly felt — was totally misplaced, having to do with a vulnerable little girl inside, not with the strong CEO she'd become. That's what I mean by self-awareness.

The fundamentally self-confident CEOs I've worked with and observed have embodied a character trait that I think of as true humility. They are so secure, psychologically speaking, that they are able to celebrate — and capitalize on — the strengths of the people around them, both board and staff members. They're blessed with robust, healthy egos that aren't easily wounded and don't require constant protection. They are able to keep things in perspective, seldom seeing a personal challenge, slight or even insult as a cause célèbre. Rather, they are able to take the long view, resisting the impulse to lash out now in the interest of achieving an important objective down the pike. They're keenly aware that the person who's treated them with apparent disrespect today might very well turn out to be a valuable ally someday if they bide their time.

Virginia Jacko, my colleague and coauthor of our book, *The Blind Visionary*, is a great example of a fundamentally self-confident CEO who's wasted absolutely zero time defending a fragile ego. President & CEO of the Miami Lighthouse for the Blind and Visually Impaired, Virginia, who is blind, recounts a story in our book that vividly demonstrates the value of a healthy ego. Not long after her appointment as the first blind CEO of the Miami Lighthouse, Virginia learned that a prominent Lighthouse volunteer had commented to a current Lighthouse board member, referring to her appointment, "Can you believe the inmates are now running the asylum?" Were Virginia's feelings hurt? Of course. Did she lash out in anger? Of course not. She didn't take any action, and when she eventually sat down in a meeting with her detractor, she made clear her desire to work together, letting bygones be bygones. The upshot? The person who'd made the derogatory comment became a close ally, even nominating Virginia for a major community award. That's the kind of emotional maturity that makes Virginia a highly successful out-of-the-box leader.

KEY WORK OF THE INNOVATOR-IN-CHIEF

Leading the out-of-the-box change charge as your organization's Innovator-in-Chief, the CEO plays three key roles that are critical to accomplishing significant change in your organization:

- As **Chief Process Designer**, the vision-driven CEO makes sure that the structures and processes that are required to plan and implement out-of-the-box change are well designed, both technically (for example, the planning steps that board members, staff, and external stakeholders go through actually result in technically sound change initiatives that can be implemented) and from a psychological/political perspective (for example, participation in the planning process turns key stakeholders into owners of out-of-the-box change initiatives and consequently change champions for those initiatives).

- As **Chief Motivator**, the change-savvy CEO employs her words and deeds — usually in person and always very visibly — to build support for, and commitment to, out-of-the-box change, countering the inevitable inertia and resistance that work against successful change.

- As **Chief Enabler**, the out-of-the-box leader enables the change process to move forward from plans to action in a full and timely fashion, through clear and firm direction, incisive decision making, the allocation of sufficient resources in terms of both staff time and money, and — when necessary — disciplinary action to overcome efforts to sabotage change.

THE CEO AS CHIEF PROCESS DESIGNER

How's this for a great scenario?

> *Day-to-day operations at the headquarters of your international association are humming along with nary a hitch. Distractions are at a minimum and no crises are looming on the horizon. Indeed, the administrative organization is on autopilot, and so you, the president & CEO, and your executives and managers have oodles of time to concentrate on accomplishing the kind of out-of-the-box change that you know is essential to future stability, security, and growth, such as launching major new programs for your members and significantly strengthening ties with key stakeholders in your environment. Not only is time an abundant commodity, but you've got an unrestricted fund for significant innovation amounting to $10 million, so you can move full steam ahead with out-of-the-box planning without any resource worries.*

Sounds good, doesn't it? But does it describe your situation these days? Probably not. Whether you're leading and managing a hospital, college, international association, school district, or public transportation authority — whatever — time is almost certainly at a premium. Meeting day-to-day demands, solving one operational problem after another, and reacting to the occasional unanticipated crisis probably take the great majority of your CEO's and managers' time (95 percent sound about right?), and if you have an unrestricted innovation fund of $50,000, or even $20,000, you're indeed fortunate.

My point isn't that life is cruel; it's that getting out of the day-to-day box to focus on planning and implementing significant change initiatives will find you swimming against a powerful current that's always threatening to take you along with it, overwhelming your change efforts in the process. The solution? To be sure, focus, discipline, and tenacity will help. But the fundamental answer is the conscious, meticulous design of planning and implementation process and structure. Design determines who will do what, when — and how will they be organized to do it — in fashioning and implementing out-of-the-box change initiatives. The detailed design of process and structure is the only way to ensure that typical organizations (as opposed to the highly fortunate few) — those contending with all kinds of pressures, distractions, and crises without the benefit of oodles of spare time and cash on hand to invest — are able to beat the odds and get out-of-the-box change successfully accomplished.

So, you might be asking, what does something that sounds so technical — process design — have to do with our organization's CEO? Why do you call her the Chief Process Designer? Isn't designing out-of-the-box planning and implementation processes something you'd normally delegate to a chief operating officer (COO) or planning director? Well, my experience has taught me that only your CEO has the organizational clout to get a new process firmly established and to compel participation in that process, and that's doubly true of any "newstream" process (to use Harvard Business School Professor Rosabeth Moss Kanter's term) that bucks the day-to-day operational tide. As Chief Process Designer in your organization, the CEO doesn't have to do every last bit of the design job; there's plenty of detailed work for a COO or planning director to do on the design front. But your CEO must be the hands-on-the-wheel driver of process design, making sure that a workable process and structure are put in place. This means knowing, in detail, the outcomes that you want the process and structure to achieve and making sure that the process is both:

- **Technically feasible** (Will going through the motions actually produce feasible, affordable out-of-the-box change initiatives that can be implemented?); and
- **Psychologically and politically sound** (Are the most critical stakeholders involved at the right points in the process, so that their participation is not only meaningful but also breeds feelings of ownership that will transform them into change champions?)

In the following chapter, I deal with the technical steps involved in coming up with out-of-the-box change initiatives to be added to your organization's Change Investment Portfolio, so I want to focus on the psychological and political aspect of design here. Wearing the Process Designer hat, your organization's Innovator-in-Chief has a preeminent design goal on the psychological/political front: to generate change champions who will play a major role in countering organizational inertia and normal human resistance to change. Your CEO can ensure the generation of change champions in two major ways: first, by designing the planning process so that it breeds feelings of ownership via participation in shaping out-of-the-box change initiatives and, second, by the CEO's motivating and inspiring staff and other stakeholders through both words and deeds.

Ownership is an extraordinarily powerful human feeling that not only fuels commitment to a thing or a course of action that's owned, but also releases tremendous positive energy. Audiences for finished staff work are just that: audiences. They might really appreciate, and even admire, a beautifully crafted, handsomely bound plan, but their role is basically passive/reactive, which is at the opposite pole from ownership. Passive/reactive audiences don't have the makings of change champions, who are created through meaningful participation in shaping — not reacting to — change that they own.

I'm reminded of a board member of a public transportation authority that was a client of mine a decade or so ago. A retired CEO who was a highly committed and dedicated board member, this fellow was tremendously negative toward me when I appeared on the scene to assist in planning and facilitating a daylong strategic work session for the authority. His answers during the telephone interview I conducted were terse, to put it mildly, and he radiated hostility. So the tremendously change-savvy CEO and I came up with a ministrategy: Put this resident critic and curmudgeon on the agenda development committee for the work session and also make sure that he led the very important breakout group that would identify opportunities and challenges looming on the authority's horizon. I'm sure you can guess the result. The resident curmudgeon, although still quite curmudgeonly (no brain transplant was attempted!), became a strong owner of the changes that resulted from the retreat and a passionate change champion for their implementation.

Let's take a larger scale example on the planning process front. A key step in planning out-of-the-box change that I describe in detail in the following chapter of this book is updating your organization's strategic framework — its core values and vision for the long-range future. You can obviously approach this job in a number of ways, technically speaking. Your planning staff might bang out values and vision statements, which your CEO reviews, finalizes, and presents to the board for adoption early in the out-of-the-box planning process.

There's nothing inherently wrong with this approach, technically speaking, but, as you can easily see, it's hopelessly flawed from the political and psychological perspective. Indeed, a CEO who would bring finished values and vision statements to her board for adoption would rank near the bottom of the change-savvy scale.

Think about it. Values and vision are powerful planning products that drive the whole change process, and they are at such a high level that shaping them doesn't require detailed technical knowledge. What a wonderful opportunity to involve the members of your board in doing important work early in the change planning process, building their ownership of the process and turning them into change champions whose support you sorely need! So it's a no-brainer that a change-savvy CEO wearing the Chief Process Designer hat will see to it that the planning process design incorporates early board involvement in updating values and vision statements. One of the most effective ways of ensuring meaningful involvement is a daylong retreat, as I discuss in the following chapter, at which your board members, along with your executive team, brainstorm the values and vision statements, after which your board's planning committee works with the CEO and executive team in fine-tuning and finalizing the statements for presentation to the board.

Your CEO, wearing the Chief Designer hat, might also decide that key internal and external stakeholders beyond the board and executive staff should be involved in shaping the values and vision statements as a way of widening ownership of the out-of-the-box change process and adding to the cadre of change champions. The president & CEO of an international association I worked with a couple of years ago made this a planning design requirement, so two very important steps were built into the process. First, key association leaders not serving on the association board who chaired a number of non-board association technical advisory committees (for example, the annual meeting planning committee and the member certification committee) were invited to the retreat kicking off the change planning process, so they had an early opportunity to provide input on the values and vision statements. Second, the preliminary values and vision statements that had been brainstormed at the planning retreat — before being refined by the board planning committee and executive team — were run by various staff groups (for example, the member services department) to get their input.

THE CEO AS CHIEF MOTIVATOR

Even if you've put in place a technically reliable planning process for identifying out-of-the-box issues and fashioning change initiatives to address them, you can't expect to win at the change game unless you pay close attention to the psychological dimension. Above all else, it's critical that you not underestimate people's very normal and quite common resistance to change. Emotional resistance can be a tremendous barrier, principally by impeding implementation of even the most technically sound change initiatives. Who hasn't seen sullen staff resistance sink an organizational change initiative or internal resistance keep a person from accomplishing an important change goal in his or her life? I've even seen emotional resistance block people's creativity — keeping them from spotting opportunities and challenges in their environments and hindering them in coming up with possible change initiatives to deal with the issues they've recognized.

My work as an executive and consultant has taught me that many if not most people not only don't welcome change in their lives and organizations, they can be really ingenious at keeping it from happening. Why the emotional resistance to changing? It seems to me that fear is the culprit, more often than not. Many if not most people, so far as I can tell, won't readily jump on the change bandwagon because they're afraid to. This might not be true of you if you're a board member, CEO, or senior executive, but the farther you move away from the top tier of leadership in an organization, the more fear you are likely to encounter. What are staff and volunteers afraid of? For one thing: anxiety, which is anything but a comfortable feeling. Tried and true routines feel familiar, comfortable, and safe, whereas the possibility of venturing into the unknown to do something really new can feel quite dangerous and cause lots of anxiety. Perhaps the most fearsome prospect is the possibility of failing at doing something new and suffering the consequent embarrassment or even humiliation. The fact is, people are sensible to expect emotional pain when changing in important ways, which is why the old saw "no pain, no gain" makes sense.

In addition to the very normal human resistance to change that is largely fear-based, in the real world where you and I live and work, staff members and volunteers in nonprofit and public organizations are so busy and under so much pressure — not to speak of feeling pretty anxious and fearful about being jerked out of their comfort zones — that getting them to participate wholeheartedly and creatively in a new planning process is no small challenge. Of course, people can be bludgeoned into going through the motions, but grudging acquiescence isn't a recipe for the kind of creative involvement that will generate high-stakes out-of-the-box change initiatives. So the primary goal of your CEO, wearing the Chief Motivator hat, is to get your staff and volunteers to *want* to participate fully in your out-of-the-box change planning process.

Your Chief Motivator's primary tool is direct communication — preferably oral and whenever feasible, in person. The written word is a much more distant, less direct tool that is notoriously weak motivator, not only because many people tend not to pay close attention to the written word, but also because it involves far less of a commitment on your CEO's part and so makes less of an impression on people. As you no doubt know, the spoken word really can make a powerful difference, no matter how weary, scared or even cynical the audience you're speaking to, serving two important, closely related purposes in the out-of-the-box change game:

1. **Education** – Explaining to staff and volunteers:

    - *Why* it makes the best of sense for them to participate in the out-of-the-box change process — in terms of need (for example, to deal with such threats as increasing competition, declining governmental support, a dramatically changing membership composition) and benefits (for example, a more secure and competitive organization that is growing).

    - And *how* they are being asked to participate: the key elements of the planning process, the roles that staff and volunteers will play, and the timing.

In my experience, anxiety and fear go hand in hand with ignorance, and people who know in detail what to expect are much more likely to buy into a process than people who feel in the dark.

2. **Inspiration** – Building emotional commitment by appealing less to the head than the heart, raising people's sights above the proverbial trench and infusing the change process with higher meaning by interpreting current events in terms of fundamental values and overarching vision.

At the national level, two of the most effective Chief Motivators in American history were Presidents Franklin D. Roosevelt and Ronald Reagan, and their success at leading significant out-of-the-box change in their very different eras undoubtedly owes much to their being masters of oral communication. Strolling through the FDR Presidential Library at Hyde Park a few years ago after facilitating a board retreat at the Henry A. Wallace Visitor and Education Center, I stopped to listen to a recording of one of FDR's radio fireside chats. If I recall correctly, he was explaining why it was necessary for the federal government to close banks around the country temporarily as part of a national bank holiday. What an effective teacher he was, calmly — sounding like an older brother or kindly uncle — describing complex economic matters in simple terms easily understood by the average American. As I listened, I recalled my parents telling me how frightened they'd been in the early days of the Great Depression — newly married and living on the handsome income of $10 a week. The economy had ground to a halt, the future looked bleak, hope was in short supply. FDR's educational radio chats were a godsend to my parents and millions of other despairing Americans, a wonderful example of the power of carefully chosen words to allay fear and restore a sense of hope and optimism in even the direst of circumstances. As president, Ronald Reagan presided over a rebirth of American optimism and pride, after the dark years of presidential assassination, the Vietnam War, and a disgraced president who'd been forced to resign. President Reagan spoke to a nation less frightened than dispirited, and his words, eloquently spoken on many occasions, told the inspiring story of America as a beacon on the hill, radiating the promise of democracy throughout the world.

I could talk about many other master communicators whose words have had tremendous influence on the course of human events. There is Lincoln redefining the fundamental meaning of the Civil War in his brilliant address (under 300 words!) at Gettysburg on November 19, 1863, asking his fellow Americans to resolve "that this nation, under God, shall have a new birth of freedom — and that government of the people, by the people, for the people, shall not perish from the earth." And there is Dr. Martin Luther King in his stirring, unforgettable "I have a dream" speech at the Lincoln Memorial on August 28, 1963, envisioning an America that will one day "rise up and live out the true meaning of its creed: 'We hold these truths to be self-evident; that all men are created equal.' " However, I'd like to turn to some closer-to-home examples of nonprofit and public CEOs wearing the Chief Motivator hat.

The following three real-life examples of CEOs playing the role of Chief Motivator in their nonprofit and public organizations might be narrower in scope and less inspiring than the above examples on the grand national stage, but they were nonetheless tremendously important to the organizations involved in out-of-the-box change.

The setting for our first example is a convocation of the board members, department heads and managers of a large children's services agency providing residential treatment, early childhood development, and community-based prevention services. The occasion: to launch a new out-of-the-box planning initiative. The board chair opens the convocation by welcoming everyone, explaining the purpose of the meeting and introducing the board members who'd been able to attend, then turns the gavel over to the executive director. Using an attractive set of PowerPoint slides, the executive director first summarizes important conditions and trends that make up the planning context (for example, likely major reductions in state financing over the next few years; new certification requirements taking effect; growing demand for early childhood development), after which she articulates the primary goals of the new planning process (for example, to identify change initiatives aimed at ensuring financial stability and service quality; to diversify services in order to meet new needs). Then she turns to her associate executive director for planning, who, also with the aid of PowerPoint, goes step-by-step through the planning process, beginning with a daylong retreat at which the agency's mission will be updated and major issues will be identified and analyzed through the eventual formation of staff and volunteer task forces to fashion concrete change initiatives. Plenty of time is reserved for questions from the floor. The executive director sticks around for the full meeting and takes the lead in answering questions.

The setting of our second example is a meeting of task force members in conference rooms in the two cities where the state bar association offices are located, linked via video conferencing. The occasion: to get the five task forces going in fashioning out-of-the-box change initiatives in their respective areas. The CEO, speaking from a conference room in the state bar headquarters, opens the meeting by welcoming everyone and telling them how critical their task force work will be to the future of the state bar. He then sketches the history that has led to this point in the process, including the retreat that kicked off the effort and the follow-up work by the board's planning committee and the executive team, resulting in an updated vision statement and the selection of the five high-stakes issues the newly formed task forces are being asked to address. Since the majority of the people in the two conference rooms hadn't been involved in the retreat and follow-up work, the CEO spends a half hour answering questions about how they'd arrived at this point. He then turns the meeting over to his chief operating officer, who goes over the methodology that the task forces are expected to employ in fashioning their change initiatives and the schedule they'd be following.

And our third example is set in a daylong strategic work session involving the board, executive team, strategy formulation task force chairs, and selected community stakeholders (including the community college president, chamber of commerce CEO, and regional planning commission chair) of the regional public transportation authority of a major southwestern metro area. The occasion: presentation of the first-cut strategic initiatives that the task forces had developed over the past six months and the identification of needed refinements. The authority's general manager (GM), recognizing that one of the major reasons for the session was to showcase the authority's commitment to innovation and to reward task force chairs for their extraordinary effort, made sure that the session was held in an attractive, comfortable off-site location and that the occasion was as much a ceremony as a working meeting. So after the board chair welcomed everyone and explained why they'd been assembled, the GM shared the updated vision and core values statements that had provided a high-level framework for the task forces' work, taking the time to cover these critical philosophical pieces of the change puzzle point-by-point. She then made a point of introducing each of the task force chairs, providing a thumbnail professional bio, after which she reviewed the charge to each task force and the methodology they'd been asked to follow. Having set the stage, the GM turned the meeting over to the task force chairs to present their preliminary initiatives and respond to questions.

As these real-life examples demonstrate, motivating staff and volunteers isn't a matter of words alone. It's not enough just to talk; as they say, you've got to "walk the talk" as well. In this regard, the CEO's physical presence at key points in the out-of-the-box planning and implementation process is critical, signaling to everyone involved that out-of-the-box change is a top-tier CEO priority. I worked with a public school district superintendent a few years ago who, after kicking off a major planning initiative at a half-day workshop involving the school board and his top lieutenants, literally disappeared from the scene, leaving his associate superintendent for curriculum and instruction to chair key planning sessions from that point on. You'd better believe that his absence didn't go unnoticed, and his inattention really took the wind out of the planning sails after a month or so had passed. One sure sign of trouble was flagging attendance at planning task force meetings. After all, these were really smart people with enough bureaucratic experience to know that if the top guy has lost interest, there's not much of a point in losing much sleep over the process. Fortunately, the associate superintendent and I were able to convince the erring CEO to jump back into the fray, and the process got back on track before being seriously derailed.

THE CEO AS CHIEF ENABLER

Wearing her Chief Enabler hat, your organization's CEO ensures that the out-of-the-box planning and implementation process actually works as designed, by: (1) making critical decisions in a timely fashion; (2) making sure that the process is provided with adequate financial and technical support; (3) monitoring and regulating the pace of change to ensure that staff and volunteers don't become dangerously overextended; and (4) taking disciplinary action as appropriate to deal with resistance. In the decision-making arena, an example would be the CEO's reviewing and signing off on the updated values and vision statements, developed by her executive staff after the board retreat at which they were brainstormed, and their submission to the board for approval before presenting them to the planning task forces getting underway. This sounds pretty straightforward; after all, you'd expect these key decision points to be identified in the out-of-the-box planning process design, so they couldn't possibly catch anyone off guard. True, but what about a CEO who's constantly traveling as part of the job? I'm currently working with two CEOs who are seldom in the office; one heads an international professional association and the other a disabilities nonprofit with locations in seven states. Getting these peripatetic executives to make important decisions in a timely fashion isn't a piece of cake, requiring a good deal of planning and virtuoso scheduling.

Ensuring adequate financial and technical support for out-of-the-box planning and implementation activities is one of the most important roles of your CEO wearing the Chief Enabler hat, not only because inadequate resources can slow or even totally derail the change train, but also because the CEO is your organization's resource generator par excellence. And, of course, no staff member other than your CEO — often in conjunction with her board — has the formal authority to reallocate significant dollars in your organization's budget. I've recently worked with a couple of CEOs who have performed splendidly as major-league resource generators. The CEO of a blind services nonprofit, for example, took the initiative in convincing her board chair, the CEO of a major business, to personally cover the cost of a governance consultant to assist in carrying out one of the agency's highest-stakes change initiatives: significantly upgrading the board's governing capacity. Without the consulting assistance, there's no way the agency's governance task force could have accomplished so much so quickly, and there was no flexible money in the budget to cover the cost.

To take another recent example, the superintendent of one of the country's largest public school districts played a hands-on role in orchestrating the staff effort to secure major foundation funding for a far-reaching, districtwide initiative to enhance teacher effectiveness. In light of the millions of grant dollars available and the school district's pressing need to take classroom teaching up a significant notch, this aggressive Innovator-in-Chief didn't hesitate to play the leading role in getting the grant application completed over a period of three months, including actually hosting Saturday task force meetings at her home. If she'd sat back like a traditional educational administrator, issuing directives from her office and periodically responding to progress reports from the task force, a competing school district might very well have walked away with millions of dollars. That's enablement to the max!

Of course, a major, ongoing responsibility of every CEO in the world is to ensure that his or her organization is properly staffed, and that the human resource development function, including staff capacity building, is well managed. As one of the reviewers of the manuscript of this book pointed out, having the right people — in terms of knowledge and skills — in place at the right time is a critical factor in getting significant, complex organizational change accomplished. In practice, this means that a strong dose of talent assessment should be factored into the infrastructure for change.

Guarding against overextension requires paying close attention to what's happening as the out-of-the-box change process unfolds — from planning through implementation. The successful Innovator-in-Chief always manages to keep his fingers on the pulse of the organization, through frequent informal interaction (such as sitting in on task-force planning sessions every now and then as an observer) as well as via whatever formal monitoring structure and process have been put in place (for example, one of my clients has created a strategic change coordinating council that meets biweekly to monitor the work of various planning and implementation task forces). A Chief Enabler who's on top of his game is always looking for signs of stress that, if unaddressed, might dangerously slow or even disrupt the change process. He will make sure that timely action is taken to alleviate the stress.

I've seen CEOs slow down the pace of change, easing deadlines or eliminating competing priorities as a means of lowering their organization's blood pressure. And sometimes more up-close-and-personal CEO intervention is called for, including serving as in-house therapist, as my next true story illustrates. A young fellow in his late twenties was brought in from out of town to serve as the chief operating officer (COO) of a social service agency in Pennsylvania that was engaged in early childhood education, job training and placement, and community organization. The agency was going through a comprehensive redo of its financial policies and procedures, including instituting a two-week lag between the end of a two-week work period and the issuance of the biweekly paycheck for that period. This new COO's job was to oversee planning and execution of this and the other financial system reforms, which included his explaining the rationale behind the changes being made to staff and making sure implementation moved ahead despite whatever angst was being stirred up.

Fortunately for the new COO, he was teamed up with a CEO, only a year older, who recognized the need to intervene personally when the imminent new biweekly pay period got the staff, many of whom actually thought they'd be losing a chunk of their earnings, up in arms. The COO's rational explanation didn't cut ice, especially coming from an outsider with a technocratic demeanor. (He definitely wasn't hired to be Mr. Nice Guy, nor would he have fit the role.) Ben, the CEO — a warm, charismatic fellow much admired in the community not only for his tireless advocacy for the agency but also his hoop heroics during his undergraduate days at a local college — stepped in just in time.

He pulled the whole staff together at one of their community service centers and made a passionate personal appeal to go along with the changes, which, he said, were essential for the agency to command respect in the community as a well-managed nonprofit and for him to succeed as their CEO. "I've known most of you for years, and I've personally recruited many of you," he was quoted as saying. "Do you really believe I'd let you be cheated out of money you've earned? Anyone who thinks I'd do that to my own people, stand up!" No one stood. The payroll and other reforms were accomplished over the next year, but they certainly wouldn't have been — at least not nearly as smoothly — without Ben's wearing the Chief Enabler hat so effectively.

I don't have much to say about the disciplinary role of the CEO wearing her Chief Enabler hat. The overwhelming majority of the time, in my experience, when a CEO has made sure well-designed out-of-the-box change processes are put in place and staff and volunteers are appropriately motivated and provided with the financial, technical, and other support they need, there isn't a need for disciplinary action. But on those rare occasions when dysfunctional behavior threatens progress, a change-savvy CEO won't hesitate to take action. I recall such an instance, going back a decade. I was consulting with a nonprofit nursing home chain that had set up five or six planning task forces to hammer out change initiatives in their respective areas. One of the highest priority task forces, which was charged to come up with a comprehensive revenue diversification initiative, was appropriately headed by the chief financial officer, who was as competent as they come, in terms of finance, anyway. But his interpersonal relations and diplomatic genes were missing.

Only six weeks into the revenue diversification task force effort, several staff members had complained to the Executive Director/CEO, and two of the key volunteers had actually dropped out. Virtually everyone on the task force was alienated by the CFO's arrogant, often authoritarian style of leadership, and the whole effort was rapidly unraveling. CEO action was clearly called for, and it was taken. The CFO was removed from his chair role and replaced by one of the volunteers. Feelings were so raw that it wasn't possible for the CFO to serve as a full-fledged task force member. Instead, the Executive Director assigned him to coordinate staff support for the task force. By the way, not wanting to humiliate his CFO, who was a critical executive team member, the Executive Director went out of his way to come up with a public face-saver, explaining in writing and in person at the next task force meeting that tremendous financial planning demands meant that he couldn't spare his CFO for full-fledged involvement in the task force. Everyone knew what was going on, of course, but the CFO appreciated the sensitive treatment.

Chapter Two

OUT-OF-THE-BOX CHANGE PLANNING AND MANAGEMENT

A POWERFUL NEW CHANGE PLANNING TOOL

I'm happy to report good news on the planning front. In recent years a very powerful change-focused planning logic and methodology have been developed and successfully tested in all sectors — for-profit, public and nonprofit. In my work as a change consultant and in this book, I call this the Change Investment Portfolio Process (from this point on, Portfolio Process) but you can call it whatever you want; semantics aren't a passion of mine. In a nutshell, the Portfolio Process, which is run parallel to, and separate from, your organization's business-as-usual operational planning/budget development process, produces out-of-the-box change in the form of concrete projects that I call change initiatives. These change initiatives are housed in your organization's Change Investment Portfolio until they are ready to be mainstreamed into ongoing operations — or occasionally abandoned if they've proved unworkable. (See Figure 1 on page 36.)

    The change initiatives housed in your organization's Change Investment Portfolio are intended to address a small number of issues — think of them as "change challenges" — that your organization is facing, in the form of opportunities to grow — in terms of program and service diversification, revenue generation, or customers/clients

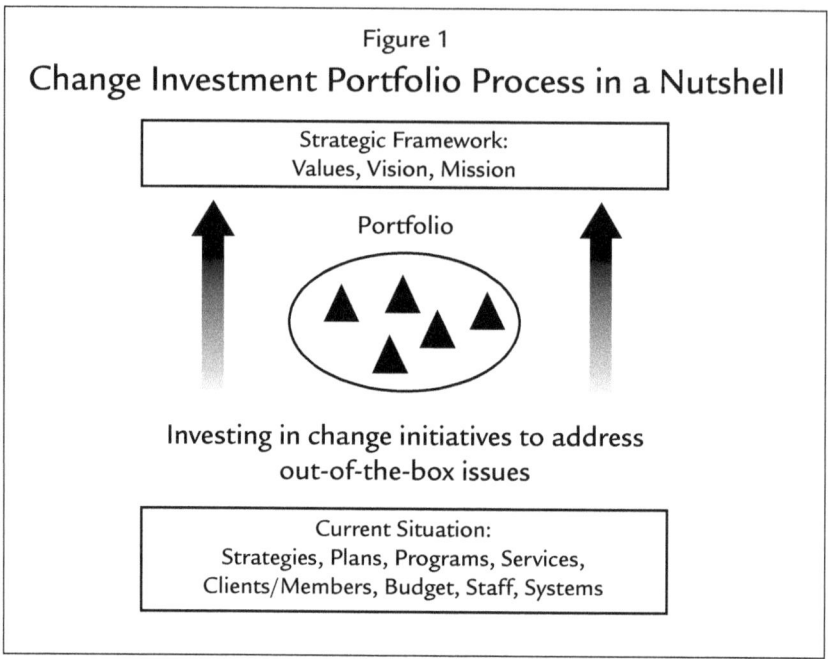

Figure 1
Change Investment Portfolio Process in a Nutshell

— and challenges and threats to your organization's future stability and growth. By far the most challenging aspect of the Portfolio Process is to select the right issues to address: the ones that are so high-stakes and so complex that you could not reasonably expect them to be handled effectively through the parallel, business-as-usual operational planning/budget development process. Never forget that your annual operational planning/budget development process is a very effective vehicle for dealing with the great majority of issues your organization is facing at any particular time, as I observe in the Overview; but there will always be issues you wouldn't want to trust to mainstream planning.

Each of the change initiatives being managed in your Change Investment Portfolio (let's call it the CIP from this point on) at any particular time will have its own time frame, which is why arbitrary cycles such as three or five years make no sense. For example, let's say that an international professional association is handling four change initiatives in its CIP right now: (1) developing and pilot testing a new member service (18 months); (2) redesigning its governance structures and processes, including the board of directors (24 months); (3) building an international presence (30 months); and (4) merging with a sister association (6 months). The Portfolio Process is by design highly selective for the simple reason that your organization's resources — in staff time, money, and technical capability — are limited. The Portfolio Process is at the opposite pole from supermarket planning lists of ten, fifteen, or more goals. In my years in the change business, I've never seen a public or nonprofit organization effectively manage more than three to five change initiatives concurrently at any given time. Of course, as change initiatives are implemented, they drop out of the CIP and are integrated into your organization's operating plan and budget, and new change initiatives are regularly added to your CIP.

Keep in mind that what I'm talking about couldn't be more different from the old-time notion of a strategic umbrella (consisting of five-year goals and strategies), within which your organization would develop its annual operating plan and budget, which in theory is tied back to the goals and strategies that your umbrella encompasses. So far as I can tell, these ties have always been more theoretical and aesthetic than practical. Instead, think of parallel processes that proceed concurrently. During every fiscal year your organization prepares next year's annual operating plan and budget (your in-the-box planning), while concurrently — but through a separate and parallel process — your organization manages change initiatives in your CIP and adds new change initiatives to your CIP to address new issues that your organization has identified. These two separate and parallel processes typically share a common starting point (usually a daylong planning retreat kicking off the annual planning cycle, which I'll discuss in detail in the next chapter) and are linked at the end by the mainstreaming/budgeting of completed change initiatives into the annual operating plan. (See Figure 2 on page 39.)

A REACTION TO THE FAILURE OF TRADITIONAL LONG-RANGE PLANNING

The Portfolio Process was developed in reaction to the obvious failure of traditional long-range strategic planning as a tool for generating significant change. Two up-close encounters with traditional long-range planning of the five-year ilk during the executive management phase of my career taught me how easily trees could be sacrificed and precious hours consumed while generating tons of paper but only the illusion of significant change. The first learning encounter happened during my tour of duty in state government. I was chief operating officer of the urban affairs division of the newly created department responsible for community and economic development in one of the five largest, most urbanized and industrialized states in the union. One of the campaign planks of the recently elected, dynamic young governor was to bring modern planning and management practices to a state government that he'd lambasted for rampant cronyism on the campaign trail. So none of us newly hired executives were surprised when a new statewide planning process was launched during his first year in office.

In a nutshell, each division was instructed to prepare a set of overall five-year goals and, within this overarching framework, to develop annual performance targets for each of the next five years related to each of the long-range goals. So as a first step, my division executive team colleagues and I fashioned our division's five-year goals state-

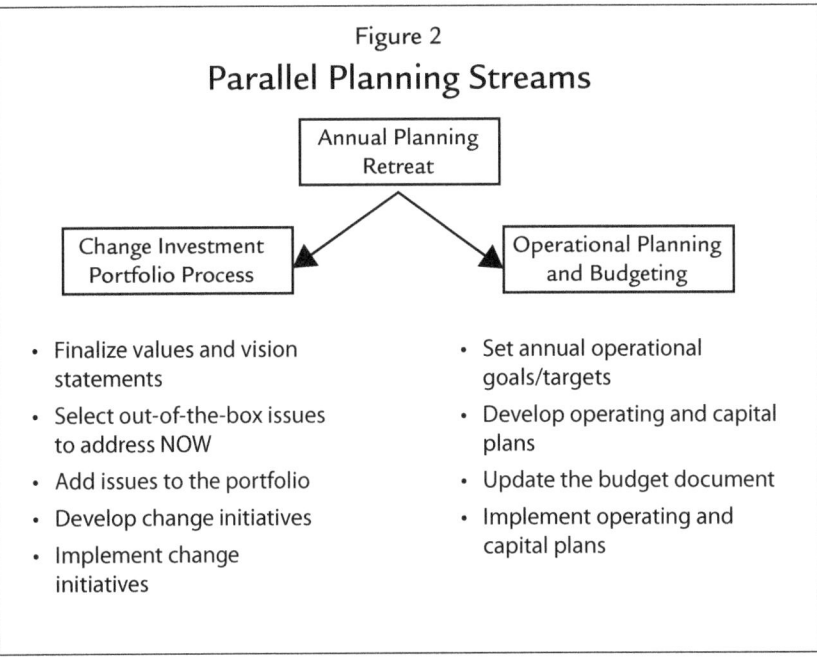

ment and mapped out performance targets for each goal for the current fiscal year. For example, under the goal of building local community action agency management capacity, one of our first-year performance targets was to provide 150 hours of technical assistance to the directors of community action agencies around the state. With the first-year targets down on paper, we then projected increased levels of effort for each target for each of the ensuing four years.

No question, having to go through the planning exercise gave all of us a firm grasp of the work of our division, so we'd developed a pretty useful management tool. What bothered all of us was how little we could say — at least with any confidence — about what would be going on in our part of the world much beyond the next year, and we quite reasonably wondered whether projecting levels of performance for years two through five would be worth the effort. I'll never forget one of our planning sessions that'd run well past dinner. We were sitting around brainstorming future performance, and it went something like this: "OK, so this year we'll be delivering × hours of technical assistance aimed at beefing up local agencies' financial management practices and systems. How does a 3 percent increase sound for the second year and 3.5 percent in year four?" At some point in the evening we realized how worthless this kind of brainstorming was, which made it a lot easier to get through the exercise and get home to dinner. Why worry about accuracy when you don't have much of a clue about the future beyond next year, and whatever you say will likely turn out to be way off base down the pike?

Well, we got our division plan submitted on time, and it was bundled along with the other division plans into a departmental strategic plan, which was then compiled into a massive statewide planning tome that must have weighed ten pounds. I'm not sure what ultimately happened to this monster document; I actually can't recall ever seeing it. What I do know is that once our division plan was put on the shelf, we never referred to it again, and I can't remember a time that we pulled it off the shelf to remind ourselves what performance projections we'd made for a particular period.

Six years or so later, I'm now executive assistant and chief of staff to the president of a large, urban community college with three campuses and, at that time if I recall correctly, around 40,000 students. I'm finally getting around to writing the paper that will make me a bona fide masters degree holder and get rid of that irritating "pending thesis" tag on my resume, and I've decided to do a study of the innovation impact of the institution's planning. For the past five years, the institution had been engaged in a comprehensive long-range planning process not that different from the one I'd been exposed to in state government. It was a rolling process that involved annually updating the projected activity in major goal areas for each of the next five years, and a similar bottom-up compilation process was employed: updated academic and administrative unit plans compiled into department plans into campus plans and ultimately into a college-wide *Five-Year Plan of Advancement*.

The first major part of my study was to identify every college investment in significant innovation over the past five years. My criteria for coming up with investments were simple: resources — both time and money — had to have been allocated to a brand new program or project that didn't exist in the current operating plan and budget and, therefore, could not be considered merely an expansion of ongoing activity. The second part of my study was to determine the source of every one of these major investments in innovation in order to assess the innovation impact of the very elaborate long-range planning process that the institution had been using for the past five years.

You won't be surprised to know that not one of the identified innovations had been generated by the comprehensive five-year planning process. How could they have been, since not one of the innovation investments had a home in any of the college's existing planning units? The sources, in every case, were creative, aggressive administrators and faculty members working outside of the formal planning process — coming up with new initiatives and then fighting for them up the line until ultimately getting them approved and funded. Indeed, the college's high-tech worker retraining center was a classic example of top-down innovation, since the president himself spearheaded its development. What did the formal comprehensive long-range planning process have to do with the initiatives? It did what these formal planning processes typically do: historical recording and validation. Far from generating innovation, the college's five-year planning process incorporated the innovations — once they'd been planned and funded — so they now had a formal home and could be projected forward into the future in the next iteration of the comprehensive plan.

I'm sure many of you reading this have had your own disappointing and unsatisfying experiences with traditional long-range or strategic planning for an essentially meaningless and arbitrary period like five years. You who have suffered through one of these processes will surely agree, with me, that wasting so much time, energy, and paper to generate virtually no important change is a tragedy in the context of always-scarce resources and of the tremendous need for creative organizational change in the face of a rapidly changing world. As far as I can tell, old-fashioned comprehensive planning of the kind I've described has largely disappeared from the for-profit sector, whose bottom line and future growth depend on taking command of out-of-the-box change, and this kind of outdated planning is definitely rapidly waning in the public and nonprofit sectors. The bad news is that you'll still find nonprofit and public organizations out there engaging in old-time long-range planning. Why, for heaven's sake?

Based on experience, I'd say there are two primary culprits: (1) a very natural human desire to feel secure and safe in a threatening world in flux and (2) the all-too-common demand of stakeholders, most notably funders such as foundations, for evidence of planning and management capacity. Unfortunately, the planning documentation itself is often seen, from the outside anyway, as the product, without funders and other stakeholders digging into the real impacts of the planning process on organizational performance. To be honest, when clients of mine have been directed by outside agencies to submit five-year plans, my advice has been to spend as little time as possible describing what they're already doing and slap on a cover page with the title *Five-Year Plan*. Don't fight the requirement, but definitely don't take it too seriously!

FOUR KEY STEPS IN THE PROCESS

Four key steps are involved in generating change initiatives that will be housed in your organization's CIP:

1. **Updating your organization's Strategic Framework**, including its core values; vision for the long-range future; and mission — creating a fundamental foundation for the planning steps that follow, in terms of: a set of overarching, predominantly ethical rules of the game to govern subsequent planning and operations; a desired end state to lend purpose and direction to the planning; and programmatic and organizational boundaries that should be crossed only after very serious consideration. Involvement in updating your organization's Strategic Framework is the preeminent means to turn your board members into ardent champions for out-of-the-box change.

2. **Identifying out-of-the-box issues or change challenges** (asking, "Should we take action to do something we're not currently doing?") in the form of opportunities to make progress in translating particular elements of your organization's vision into reality and in the form of challenges that might impede achieving particular elements of your vision.

3. **Selecting the issues that your organization intends to begin addressing** *now*, by: (1) assessing the cost of *not* taking action to deal with a particular issue (direct, out-of-pocket costs such as a damaged reputation or a financial penalty, and forgone benefits such as missing out on a major new grant opportunity); (2) estimating the likely cost of taking action (including time, money, and risk) and your organization's capacity to take action; and (3) coming up with the issues that are likely to provide the most favorable

benefit/cost ratio. These issues are added to your organization's CIP, where they are turned into change initiatives.

4. **And fashioning change initiatives in the form of nuts-and-bolts projects to address the issues your organization has selected** and adding these initiatives to your organization's CIP. This is the step that provides the greatest opportunity for involving staff and volunteers who are not members of your board or executive team and turning them into owners of, and champions for, out-of-the-box change.

Every nonprofit and public organization is unique in terms of mission, circumstances, and capabilities (such as financial resources, systems, and expertise); consequently, every organization needs to map out its own unique application of the process, spelling out accountabilities and deadlines in going through the four key steps. In developing your organization's own unique planning design, however, you will want to think in terms of the process unfolding in two major phases:

- Steps 1 and 2 are taken at the open end of what I think of as the "change funnel," typically involving your board, CEO, executive team and often other key stakeholders in a daylong strategic work session or retreat, at which a brainstorming approach is taken and premature decision making is avoided. The outcome of this first phase is a preliminary version of the updated Strategic Framework and the identification of a number of strategic issues that your organization might tackle.

- Your organization will deal with steps 3 and 4 at the narrower end of the change funnel, applying discipline in making firm decisions about the issues you will tackle and the change initiatives you will add to your CIP. For example, your organization's executive team might work with your board's planning committee in firming up your values and vision statements and identifying the highest priority issues that should be addressed now and submitting them to the board for final approval. And your organization might employ staff and volunteer task forces to fashion detailed change initiatives that will be reviewed and approved by your executive team and board planning committee before being recommended to the board for adoption.

The challenge is to avoid jumping to conclusions so early in your organization's application of the Portfolio Process that you risk missing major opportunities and challenges or make premature commitments to particular courses of action. Believe me, the number of headstrong, aggressive and impatient type As populating boards and executive ranks guarantees lots of pressure to make quick decisions and get cracking on specific change strategies, and the cost of caving in to this pressure can be extremely high.

Before looking at each of the four key steps involved in the Portfolio Process in detail, I'd like to say more about the need to tailor application of the Portfolio Process to the unique needs and circumstances of your particular nonprofit or public organization. I'd also like to touch briefly on the very important role of creativity in the Portfolio Process, especially in coming up with possibilities for change when dealing with out-of-the-box issues.

NO ONE SIZE FITS ALL

The Portfolio Process is a powerful logic and very practical methodology that can be applied in any nonprofit or public organization, whatever its mission (whether social services, economic development, public transportation, education or something else) or size in terms of staffing and budget. Even the smallest nonprofit — for example, a neighborhood development corporation with only three full-time staff and a budget under $500,000 — can apply this powerful logic and make use of this practical methodology in fashioning change initiatives to capitalize on opportunities and overcome challenges. Indeed, my small consulting firm aggressively employs the Portfolio Process as a growth tool, and we're currently managing three change initiatives in our CIP: launching a new publishing arm to generate passive income to supplement consulting revenues; developing a new, highly interactive web site dedicated to selling our newest book; and building a comprehensive social media marketing program. And in the Postscript, I'll talk about how you yourself, as an individual, can apply the logic and methodology to take command of change in your personal life and career.

However, you can't expect just to plunk the Portfolio Process down carte blanche in your organization and expect it to do the job. Tailoring the Portfolio Process to your organization's unique circumstances and needs is critical to successful application. Time and other resources are so scarce that you can't risk having the process fall apart midstream because you've asked much more of your staff than you could reasonably expect. This is where the role of your CEO wearing her Chief Designer Hat comes in. I've learned that there are frequently type As lurking around who get riled up over the thought of planning to plan (which strikes them as bureaucratic), but that's exactly what I'm talking about: coming up with a detailed plan — a design, if you will — for going through the steps involved in updating your organization's CIP, spelling out responsibilities at particular points (for example, your board members participating in a daylong retreat), and making sure that your application of the process is feasible in terms of both staff time and money. You might have to spread the process out over a longer period, or limit the number of issues you deal with at the same time, or get into less depth when analyzing particular issues — whatever — but your organization will still reap significant benefits from the Portfolio Process if you've carefully tailored the application to your unique situation.

A WORD ABOUT CREATIVITY

Creativity is such a complex subject — touching on neurology, psychology, and even spirituality — that I can't really get into it in any detail in this handbook, but I do want to say a word about its role in the out-of-the-box change process before getting into the detailed steps involved in fashioning change initiatives for your CIP. As a starter, keep in mind that there's no universally accepted definition of "creative" or "creativity," nor is there agreement on the factors that influence a person's or organization's creative capacity: Whether and to what extent it's God-given, inherited, teachable and learnable is debatable and, believe me, heatedly debated. Based on my reading and hands-on experience, allow me to suggest a working definition that you can put to use in the process of updating your organization's CIP: Creativity is the capacity of your staff and volunteers to envision what doesn't currently exist — to see what isn't — in terms of possible courses of action, relating to programs, services, customers/clients, partnerships and alliances, and financial and other resources. Put differently, strengthening your organization's creative capacity expands your opportunities for out-of-the-box change.

By the above definition, it would make good sense for your CEO, wearing the Chief Designer hat, along with her top lieutenants, to build into the design of your organization's application of the Portfolio Process some practical steps to foster creative thinking. In this regard, you might want to consider building in some formal education and training for your staff in creative thinking. In thinking this through, you'll want to check into the very impressive work being done at the Center for Creative Leadership, headquartered in Greensboro, North Carolina. While the Center might be the gold standard in the field of creativity education and training, you're well advised to check into training programs that might be available at your local postsecondary institutions.

Even without any formal training, you can build into your planning process tried-and-true tools for opening people's minds, expanding their capacity to see what isn't. One of the most powerful that I've seen in practice is the daylong retreat in a comfortable, off-site location that involves lots of brainstorming in breakout groups. In the hands of a capable facilitator, a free-flowing breakout group exercise — focused on, say, identifying opportunities and challenges in the environment — can within as little as an hour expand all participants' horizons, surfacing issues that no single individual would have come up with. And the CEO, as Innovator-in-Chief of your organization, is responsible for establishing clear guidelines to prevent the exercise of premature discipline in the process of fashioning change initiatives. Let's say that a task force involving staff and volunteers in your children's services nonprofit is exploring potential initiatives to generate earned income from business enterprises of one kind or another (for example, a thrift shop or art studio). A change-savvy Innovator-in-Chief would make sure that the detailed design of the task force effort includes ample opportunity for open, free brainstorming early in the process so that the full range of possibilities is considered, rather than forcing premature choice.

STEP #1: UPDATING THE STRATEGIC FRAMEWORK

First and foremost, your organization's Strategic Framework — consisting of its core values, its vision, and its mission — provides participants with fundamental rules of the game to guide the planning process, long-range directions in the form of a desired end state to shoot for, and programmatic and structural boundaries that shouldn't be penetrated without serious second thoughts. Before looking at the three elements making up your Strategic Framework, I want you to keep some key points in mind. First, not only does your organization's updated values statement provide your planning process with fundamental guidelines, but your updated vision statement also plays a powerful role in the identification of issues, which you can think of as major opportunities to make progress in translating particular vision elements into operating reality and major challenges standing in the way of achieving particular vision elements.

Values, vision, and mission are the unique preserve of your board, CEO and senior executives, which is to say that updating them is a top-down activity. Reaching agreement on the fundamentals at this level early in the change planning process is one of the tried-and-true ways to prevent the process from breaking down midstream because of serious ideological/philosophical differences. And because values, vision, and mission are very high-level matters that tend to be philosophical in nature, rising well above technical and operational detail, updating your organization's Strategic Framework lends itself to intensive board involvement, usually in a retreat setting, and such involvement is one of the surest ways to turn board members into owners of, and champions for, out-of-the-box change.

You should be aware that it's all too easy, when dealing with the Strategic Framework of your organization, to confuse serious planning, on the one hand, with public relations and staff motivation, on the other.

You've probably been advised numerous times that the ideal vision statement is a pithy paragraph no more than two or three sentences long. Well, if you're talking about educating and inspiring the general public and key external stakeholders and motivating your staff, that's certainly true. But for serious change planning purposes, the more detailed your vision statement, the better able you will be to identify strategic issues and fashion change initiatives, as I'll explain a bit later.

And, finally, you're well advised to expect a high degree of discomfort and perhaps even some emotional resistance from board and executive team members when you involve them in updating detailed values and vision statements, for three primary reasons in my experience. For one thing, I've come across more than a few board members and executives over the years who've had a terrible experience with the pithy paragraph approach to visioning. I vividly remember one board member who, when I was interviewing him in preparation for an upcoming retreat, leveled a steely gaze at me and said without a hint of a smile, "If you force us to go through one of those excruciating exercises spending a whole morning crafting a one-paragraph vision statement, like we did last year, I'll make sure you're ridden out of town on a rail!" Be assured that I didn't, and I wasn't! Of course, discomfort is almost inevitable when you're grappling with something as abstract and philosophical as values and vision statements, which most people don't spend much time thinking about in their day-to-day lives. And finally, if you really dig into values and vision statements, you're inevitably going to surface some pretty fundamental potential conflicts that many people would feel more comfortable papering over. In reality, surfacing competing values and potentially conflicting elements of a vision statement are two of the most important reasons for updating your values and vision statements, as I'll explain below, but don't expect people to enjoy the process.

CORE VALUES

Core values define your nonprofit or public organization in terms of the fundamental principles and beliefs that you cherish. They guide and constrain your organization's planning and operations, by establishing standards — often of an ethical nature — that your organization is committed to upholding in practice and behavioral boundaries within which your organization is committed to functioning (the *thou shalt not's*). They answer the question, "What are the most important beliefs that should govern our organization?" Here are some real-life examples from retreats I've facilitated:

- A **school district** believes in "educating the whole child, in terms of both intellect and character"; "active parental involvement in the educational process"; "transparency in the governing process"; and "taking accountability for measurable educational outcomes."

- A **public transportation agency** believes in "reliable, on-time service"; "rider safety and security"; "close cooperation and collaboration with local governments and the business community"; and "the prudent management of public resources."

- An **international trade association** "values highly the competitiveness of our member companies"; "believes in active volunteer involvement in our planning and operations"; and "believes that members' needs should drive development of our services."

- And a **local economic development corporation** values statement includes constraints on growth, such as "not launching initiatives that might jeopardize our corporation's financial stability" and "not pursuing grant funding for activities outside of our basic mission," and such internal cultural norms as "a change-friendly internal atmosphere" and a "strong commitment to leadership development."

It's inevitable, if you take the process of mapping out core values very seriously, that your organization will identify core values that conflict or compete with each other. Being aware of such tensions early in the change planning process alerts your board members, CEO, and senior executives to the possible need to reconcile value conflicts as change initiatives are fashioned. Tackling such reconciliation explicitly is almost always preferable to papering over conflict that can sabotage the process farther downstream. I'm reminded of a local community development corporation I worked with that operated a revolving loan fund to finance housing rehabilitation in an older, inner-ring suburb with an aging housing stock. The prime targets for assistance were single parents economically unable to keep their properties in good shape without financial assistance. The values statement that the board, CEO, and executive team hammered out in a daylong work session surfaced a classic values conflict: a humanitarian value on the one hand — getting help to people needing it as fast as possible without needless red tape — and a business-like value on the other — making sure that loans were repaid on time and in full, with interest. As it turned out, the change initiative aimed at reforming the loan process managed to reconcile these two competing values, simultaneously expediting the loan process and strengthening the repayment process to ensure full and timely repayment.

VISION

Your organization's vision is a detailed, multifaceted picture of the future you aspire to create over the long run, in terms of:

- Your organization's **business model and structure** (for example, "Generating at least 30 percent of our annual operating budget from earned income produced by for-profit enterprises"; "Growing significantly through mergers with sister associations"; "Moving away from direct service delivery to delivering services via contracting with outside companies"; "Having facilities within a 30-minute commute for every county resident;" "Having member chapters in every one of the top 50 cities in the world"; "Building principals will be true CEOs of their buildings.")

- Your organization's **programs, products and services** (for example: "Fifty percent of our educational services will be in the form of distance learning"; "Our regional transportation network will include light rail as well as bus service"; "We will encompass the whole continuum of senior services, from senior centers to a skilled nursing home"; "We will expand our residential service capacity by 30 percent"; "Active recruitment of business prospects will at least equal advertising in terms of resource commitment"; "A nationally respected research institute will be fully operating.")

- Your organization's **clients and customers** (for example, "Our membership will double through international expansion in Asia and Latin America"; "The number of associate members paying higher dues than our regular members will increase by 15 percent"; "Adults will increase from 35 to 60 percent of our client base"; "Businesses in our community will be paying customers for worker retraining efforts"; "Small business owners will be a prime target for technical assistance.")

- Your organization's **image and external relationships** (For example: "Our agency will be seen as a critical player in the economic development arena statewide"; "We will have a close, collaborative partnership with the business community"; "Voters will support our operating and capital tax levies, seeing them as an essential investment in the community's quality of life"; "City and county governments in our region will understand and support our mission"; "We will be seen as the single most important resource for worker retraining in the community.")

- And also in terms of the **major impacts/outcomes that you want to result from carrying out your mission** (For example, "Significantly less traffic congestion and faster commutes to work"; "a more diverse business sector that includes manufacturing and financial services, in addition to tourism"; "A significant increase in our members' average annual income"; "Steadily increasing real property values"; "At least 25 percent of our college graduates return to live in the community.")

MISSION

While your organization's values and vision statements are basically aspirational — painting a picture of the organizational future you're aiming for — and, in summary form, are intended to raise sights and to motivate and inspire your staff, external stakeholders, and the wider world — your mission statement is basically a description of what your organization is right now, in terms of your structure, your programs and services, and your clients and customers. Your mission statement is an educational tool, telling people exactly who you are and distinguishing you from other organizations in the environment. It is also a disciplinary tool, keeping your organization's activities within well-defined boundaries. The mission statement of Astor Services for Children and Families, headquartered in Rhinebeck, New

York, is an excellent example: "Astor is committed to providing high-quality treatment and child development services for youngsters and their families in the least restrictive setting and at the earliest possible point of intervention. To this end, we operate a wide range of community-based and residential behavioral health treatment programs as well as early childhood development and parenting programs at multiple locations throughout our service region."

How do your organization's vision and mission statements fit together? Basically, over time as your organization's vision of what it wants to be and the impact it aspires to create expands, your mission will be pressured to change, pushing out the boundaries that define your organization. So you can think of vision as the driver of your organization's change, leading over time to an expanded mission. In this sense, revising your mission is a normal part of capitalizing on growth opportunities through launching change initiatives. However, you want your organization's mission to have a feel of permanence, and you don't want to tamper with it lightly; otherwise, there'd be a clear and present danger of your organization's running around like the proverbial headless chicken in pursuit of growth opportunities and coming to grief. So think of your mission as a valuable brake on growth and change, forcing you to have second thoughts before launching one innovation initiative or another.

STEP #2: IDENTIFYING OUT-OF-THE-BOX ISSUES

You can think of an issue as a major opportunity to make significant progress in translating one element or another of your detailed vision for the future into reality or as a major challenge or barrier standing in the way of progress in achieving your vision. Issues come in various forms. They can relate to traditional business strategy — products, services, customers, clients, and revenues — and might include: an opportunity for your community college to attract new adult learners for customized job training; a change in Medicare regulations that threatens your nursing home's bottom line; the rapid growth in your community of a minority population with serious literacy needs that challenges your library to develop an aggressive outreach program; a rapid decline in volunteer time that jeopardizes the programs of your civic association; a huge new Ford Foundation grant program that challenges your association to diversify into a new product line that might be financed by the program, and so on.

Issues can relate to image and external relations, for example: a continuing series of highly critical articles in the local paper that threatens to seriously damage your transit system's reputation and even jeopardize passage of the sales tax increase to finance the proposed new light rail system; a sister association in the rapidly consolidating insurance industry that proposes a merger with your association that might ensure long-term stability, and perhaps even growth; a deteriorating relationship with a key stakeholder, the board of county commissioners, whose opposition will seriously limit your economic development corporation's work in revitalizing the waterfront area.

And they can relate to internal leadership and management, for example: rapid turnover on your foundation's board of directors that appears to indicate extreme dissatisfaction with your board's governing structure and process; an antiquated financial management system that is causing key funders to doubt the wisdom of investing further in your nonprofit; a program staff near mutiny over personnel management problems that have simmered for years; a long-range planning process that produces far more paper than serious change and is without question causing your nonprofit to miss opportunities for growth and diversification in a highly competitive environment.

A daylong strategic work session (or retreat) is a tried-and-true vehicle for issue identification via breakout groups employing a free-flowing brainstorming process. These groups will draw on three major sources in making a list of issues from which your organization can choose the ones to address during the current planning cycle: (1) a review of major conditions and trends in your organization's external environment that are pertinent to your mission (demographic; economic; social/cultural; political/legislative; funding); (2) an assessment of internal strengths and weaknesses (related to leadership, including governance; management; financial and human resources; culture); and (3) evidence of major gaps between your formally espoused core values and actual practice.

STEP #3: SELECTING THE ISSUES TO BE ADDRESSED

In my experience as a retreat facilitator, your board, CEO and executive team will come out of the daylong work session with a list of fifteen to thirty issues of all shapes and sizes to choose from. The challenge is to decide two things: which issues from the list you've developed are out-of-the-box in the sense that it wouldn't be feasible to try to deal with them via the mainstream operational planning/budget development process, and which ones should your organization tackle during the current planning cycle. Remember: time, money, and other resources are finite and typically very scarce, especially in the nonprofit world. Your model is not General Motors' deciding to invest $2 billion in a huge new plant. You should instead conjure up a picture of a local social service agency, college, hospital, or national association with 95 percent or more of its financial resources tied up in ongoing operations, with limited opportunity to raise capital, and with a staff up to their eyeballs in work. In reality, your nonprofit will be quite fortunate to be able to tackle two or even three major change initiatives at any given time. In the change game, selectivity is the major determinant for success.

It would be a mistake to try to narrow the list of issues down to a select few at the daylong strategic work session. More time and analysis are essential to making the right selection. One approach that works very well is to hold three follow-up half-day work sessions:

- **A meeting of the CEO and executive team** for the purpose of analyzing the issues that were identified at the retreat, dividing them into two lists: (1) the issues that can be fed into the annual operational planning/budget preparation process; and (2) the issues that are out-of-the-box in the sense that they are too complex and/or high-stakes to handle through mainstream planning.

- **A second half-day meeting of the CEO and executive team** for the purpose of analyzing the list of out-of-the-box issues to determine the short list of issues to be tackled this year.

- **A half-day work session of your board's planning committee**, at which the CEO and Executive Team present their analysis and recommendations, and the Planning Committee agrees on the out-of-the-box issues to be recommended to the board for action this year.

Coming up with the short list of out-of-the-box issues to be dealt with during the current planning cycle involves asking three really tough questions for each issue.

First: What costs will our nonprofit likely incur if we do *not* tackle this particular issue over the coming year? Costs can be in the form of lost opportunity (for example, failing to secure a new funding source; missing the opportunity to capture a new market) or direct penalties for not acting (for example, loss of a current funding source; a tarnished reputation; internal chaos). At one side of the spectrum are issues that do not demand attention this year; nothing really serious will be lost by not acting. These are set aside in your nonprofit's tomorrow file — for consideration again next year. At the other end of the spectrum are issues affecting your nonprofit's very existence. These automatically make the short list. For the ones in the middle, the analysis must continue.

Second: What is the likely cost of dealing with this particular issue over the coming year, in terms of time, money, and political capital?

And third: What is the likelihood that our nonprofit can develop the capacity to deal with this particular issue, in light of the costs we anticipate? The bottom-line outcome of this analysis is a short list of out-of-the-box issues that appear to provide your nonprofit or public organization with the most favorable balance between anticipated benefits and costs. These are added to your organization's CIP, where change initiatives are developed to address them.

STEP #4: FASHIONING CHANGE INITIATIVES TO ADDRESS THE SELECTED ISSUES

Once you've selected the out-of-the-box issues for inclusion in your organization's CIP, you've traveled ninety yards down the field in the change game, since fashioning change initiatives involves straightforward project planning that nonprofit and public organizations have been doing for years, employing whatever approaches fit the particular issues you've chosen to tackle: delegation to a staff member; a task force consisting of staff and volunteers; retention of a consultant to work with a task force; and the like. Each change initiative should consist of at least the following critical elements:

- **A thorough description of the issue being addressed**, including any major sub-issues (for example, the issue is a dysfunctional board not coming close to reaching its governing potential; sub-issues include board composition; board governing work; board structure; and the board-CEO working relationship).

- **A set of specific objectives to be achieved by the change initiative** (for example, addressing the issue of a negative image in the community might involve working on three major objectives: (1) to promote wide public understanding of our mission; (2) identify and build solid working relationships with the top five stakeholder organizations in the community; and (3) engage board and executive team members systematically in representing our agency in the community.

- **A detailed work plan, identifying precisely what needs to be done, when** — including the assignment of accountability and a timeline — for the completion of each of the components involved in the change initiative.

- **The specification of the human and financial resources required** to carry out the change initiative.

- **The identification of measurable performance targets** that can be employed in assessing the success of the change initiative in meeting its objectives.

- **And a revenue/expenditure budget** for the change initiative, identifying specific sources of revenue and laying out required expenditures by particular cost categories.

A staff and/or volunteer task force can be a very effective vehicle for fashioning a change initiative, provided that: (1) the task force is provided with a clear, detailed charge from your organization's CEO, making clear the issue to be addressed, the methodology to be employed, the format of the change initiative, and the deadline for its completion; (2) a task force leader is chosen who has demonstrated strong project planning and management skills, commands the respect of colleagues, is passionate about the issue being addressed, and has successful experience as a facilitator of complex processes; (3) the work of the task force is overseen by a senior body of some kind (for example, a steering committee of senior executives), which monitors task force progress, identifies problems, and takes corrective action as appropriate (for example, replacing one or more task force members); and (4) the task force is provided with strong technical support, by staff and/or a consultant.

MANAGEMENT AND COORDINATION

Up to now this chapter has focused on the out-of-the-box planning process — from updating values and vision and identifying and selecting issues to address, to fashioning the change initiatives that are housed and managed in your organization's CIP. You can easily see that coordinating these complex activities, keeping them under control and on track, is a tremendous management challenge requiring not just a well-designed planning methodology but also a formal management structure. Without formal structure and well-defined management and coordination functions, there would be a clear and present danger of activities spinning out of control or being overwhelmed by the inexorable pressures of day-to-day operations. The price of not formally managing change through a well-defined structure can be tremendously high, as a fellow I know learned a few years ago, when he was offered the position of project manager for an ambitious, politically and technically complex, and demanding change initiative that was in the process of being implemented when he came on board.

The project involved the redesign, automation, and integration of the financial management systems of two completely independent public entities in the same metropolitan area. Both entities were committed to reaping the benefits of advanced technology, while realizing the cost savings of consolidation. Included as subsystems were budget preparation, accounting, and financial reporting. Consulting assistance was provided by a major accounting firm (one of what was then the Big Eight), but relatively junior level consultants did most of the work with little oversight and supervision. Several staff task forces were charged to design large pieces of the system, including revenue collection and accounts payable, and mountains of documentation were being generated. Before the new project manager arrived on the scene, the task forces and consulting team had been somewhat casually coordinated by an overworked management team member of one of the public entities, who had barely enough time to do his regular job, much less oversee such a complex and costly change effort as this one.

The inevitable result was chaos and near-collapse. As the newcomer on the scene, hired late in the game to serve as overall project manager, my colleague couldn't make heads or tails of what was going on. Convinced that the project was a technical abomination quickly heading toward a highly visible disaster that was likely to destroy the careers of many people associated with it — including the new project manager's — he was able to convince the higher-ups to stop the project, dismiss the consulting firm, rebid the project, retain another firm, develop detailed project objectives and an implementation plan, and create a structure to provide rigorous coordination and quality control. Eventually, the project got back on track, but only after hundreds of wasted hours, thousands of wasted dollars, and tremendous anxiety, all because of inadequate attention to management and coordination structure.

The needless risk, waste and anxiety could have been avoided by taking four straightforward steps that have been thoroughly tested in practice:

1. **Create a formal, permanent program** — in effect, a special-purpose organization within the wider organization — to house your organization's "newstream," out-of-the-box-change planning and implementation activities. This program, which your organization might brand with an appropriate title, such as the Innovation Investment Program, will protect the out-of-the-box change process from the pressures of day-to-day-operations, while focusing explicit attention on managing and coordinating the development and implementation of change initiatives in your organization's CIP.

2. Within this formal program, **establish a steering committee** to oversee and direct the program. Preferably chaired by your organization's CEO, the steering committee typically consists of the CEO's top lieutenants making up her executive team, but some clients of mine have added the board chair and vice chair. The primary purpose of the steering committee is to serve as the oversight and policy body of the change program. Its functions include: overseeing development of, and adopting, an annual comprehensive action plan charting out the work of the various task forces that are engaged in fashioning and implementing the change initiatives that are housed in the CIP; overseeing and monitoring program progress and keeping the board updated

on developments; making sure that resources are allocated to the change initiatives in a timely fashion; resolving any policy questions that might arise; and determining when implementation of particular change initiatives has advanced enough for them to be taken out of the CIP and mainstreamed.

3. **Designate a senior executive to serve as program coordinator**, typically on a part-time basis as an addition to her regular assignment (an extra hat to wear). The program coordinator is the hands-on executive responsible for day-to-day program operations, ensuring that everything is on schedule and resolving operational issues as they come up. The program coordinator also provides staff support to the steering committee, making sure that committee meetings are scheduled as needed, preparing agendas and other documentation for meetings, monitoring program progress and briefing the committee regularly, and the like. The responsibilities associated with accomplishing out-of-the-box change are so complex, demanding, and high-stakes that only an executive-level person should be assigned this role, which goes well beyond routine administrative assistance. Key attributes that make for a successful coordinator include: a passionate interest in, and commitment to, change; outstanding project planning and management skills; strong written and oral communication skills; and compatibility with the CEO.

4. And **spell out the oversight role of the board** in detail, including the specific responsibilities of the pertinent board committees. Note that the program steering committee normally periodically reports program progress via the appropriate board committee to the full board.

Chapter Three

INTENSIVE GOVERNING BODY INVOLVEMENT

COMPELLING REASONS

Getting the board actively involved in your organization's Portfolio Process, especially at the open end of the change funnel, when you're brainstorming updated values and vision statements and identifying opportunities and challenges, will pay big dividends. After this point in the process, as the funnel narrows, you'll want hands-on, intensive board involvement to give way to higher-level board engagement, primarily overseeing progress, reviewing key planning products (such as the list of recommended issues to focus on during the current planning cycle), and monitoring the implementation of change initiatives. There are three compelling reasons to make sure your board is intensively engaged early in the Portfolio Process.

First, your board members are uniquely qualified to provide critical substantive input early in the change planning process, when your organization is focusing on its Strategic Framework and the issues that deserve your organization's serious attention in the near term. It's easy to take for granted — and if you're not careful, fail to fully capitalize on — the tremendous resources board members bring to the change game, such as diverse, in-depth leadership and executive experience, knowledge and expertise in all kinds of fields such as finance and law, status and credibility in the wider world, connections with key stakeholders, including funders and potential joint-venture partners, and even occasionally the personal financial wherewithal to contribute to the change effort. As I'll discuss later, the more diverse your organization's board, the richer the reservoir of resources you'll be able to tap in the Portfolio Process, and the sounder your ultimate change initiatives are likely to be.

Second, no matter how change-savvy your organization's CEO is, and how enthusiastically and effectively she plays the Innovator-in-Chief role, she can't possibly get out-of-the box change accomplished without strong and steady board support throughout the Change Portfolio Process. For one thing, formal board review and approval confers indispensable legitimacy to such critical planning outcomes as updated values and vision statements, the issues to be added to the CIP, and the change initiatives that have been fashioned to address the issues, laying a stronger foundation for accomplishing out-of-the-box change. For another, virtually 100 percent of boards possess the power of the purse, which means they must formally allocate the dollars required to carry out change initiatives. And finally, it's a rare Innovator-in-Chief who doesn't at one time or another in the process need board backing in dealing with staff and volunteer resistance to change. It's important to keep in mind that commitment depends more on feelings of ownership than any other factor, and that the single best way to turn a key stakeholder such as your board into an owner is early involvement in shaping whatever it is you want owned. If your organization gets the board involved late in the Portfolio Process, when hands-on input isn't feasible, then you can't reasonably expect the board to feel firmly committed to the change initiatives in your CIP.

And third, the Change Investment Portfolio Process is so high-stakes in the context of our rapidly changing world — indeed, the preeminent key to your organization's long-term stability and growth — and the work involved in updating your organization's CIP is so complex and challenging, that I think of the Portfolio Process as the gold standard for board engagement. I've found that board members inevitably find dealing with such heady matters as updating values and vision and identifying issues fascinating, energizing, and tremendously satisfying. One of the important outcomes of such involvement at the open end of the change funnel is, therefore, a more solid board-CEO working relationship, since productively engaged, satisfied board members inevitably make for better partners. Also keep in mind that the absence of early, meaningful board involvement in the Portfolio Process is a recipe for resentment and even alienation of board members, who cannot help but notice that they're being consigned to the periphery of an exciting, highly important planning initiative.

LAYING THE FOUNDATION FOR BOARD INVOLVEMENT

The term "board development" describes the process of building your board's governing capacity by developing (1) the people serving on the board; (2) the governing role and work of the board; (3) the board's governing structure; and (4) the board chair-CEO working relationship. A fully developed board that's capable of doing the kind of high-impact governing work that makes a significant difference in organizational affairs is far more likely to participate successfully in planning and implementing out-of-the-box change. This might strike you as somewhat counterintuitive. I've frequently come across the notion over the years that strategic planning should always be tackled before worrying about the board's governing capacity. But the reverse is definitely true. If your board isn't well developed at the get-go, involvement in out-of-the-box change isn't likely to be nearly as productive and satisfying a governing experience.

Every successful board development initiative that I've been involved with as a governance and change consultant has been spearheaded by the organization's CEO, wearing the Chief Board Developer hat. In fact, I've never seen a case of a board that's successfully taken the lead in developing its own governing capacity. This isn't surprising when you consider that the overwhelming majority of board members are part-time, unpaid volunteers. The average board member, who typically leads a tremendously busy life outside the board, has enough trouble making it to committee and full board meetings, much less taking the lead in developing his board's governing capacity. It falls on the CEO's shoulders to get board members interested in, and educated about, the work involved in developing the board's governing capacity, and it's the CEO who recommends a process for getting the board development work accomplished. For example, the CEO of a recent client of mine, an international association, played the key role in designing a daylong governance retreat, at which board members and the executive team identified a number of steps to strengthen the board, such as putting a new committee structure in place. And, of course, this CEO played a leading role in the process of implementing the steps that'd been agreed to. Now let's take a brief look at each of these three paths to a high-impact board that's well prepared to participate in leading out-of-the-box change.

DEVELOPING THE PEOPLE ON THE BOARD

Here's a fact I've learned from my work with hundreds of boards: The more diverse your board is in terms of its membership, the more valuable your board's contribution to your organization's out-of-the-box change process is likely to be. It's difficult to imagine having too much brainpower, knowledge, expertise, experience, connections, etc., in your boardroom when you're dealing with complex issues; more is without question better. And then you've got the symbolic aspect of diversity to consider — such things as gender, race, ethnicity, economic status — which can and often does influence the legitimacy of the change initiatives your board adds to the CIP. What this means in practice is that your organization should pay systematic, close attention to developing your board's composition on an ongoing basis.

A key step in this direction is to assign a standing board committee responsibility for developing the board as a human resource. Clients of mine have employed nominating, executive, board operations, and governance committees to get this job done. Whatever its name, one of the committee's key jobs is to develop and keep updated a detailed profile of the ideal board in terms of its composition and to consciously use the profile in recruiting board members to fill gaps of one kind or another. Let's take a real-life example: a regional economic development corporation serving three counties in a metropolitan area. The board's governance committee, in a recent meeting I sat in on, dealt with the following questions when updating the profile of the corporation's board:

- To what extent should our board reflect the population of our three counties, in terms of gender, race, and ethnicity?

- What stakeholder organizations should be represented on our board (for example, the boards of county commissioners, chambers of commerce, postsecondary institutions)?

- What is the appropriate mix of business representatives on the board (small, medium, large businesses; engaged in manufacturing, financial, legal and other services; retail)?

It's important to keep in mind that your board's composition not only affects the quality of board member involvement in planning out-of-the-box change, but also your board's contribution to implementing change initiatives in your organization's CIP. On more than one occasion over the years, for example, I've seen board members who are prominent community leaders play a major role in securing funding from key stakeholders, such as the local community foundation. And I've seen well-connected board members enlist the support of stakeholder organizations that are critical to the success of particular change initiatives. One recent example is a school board member's playing the leading role in securing a chamber of commerce board's endorsement of the school district's upcoming capital levy, and the chair of a public transportation board convincing the regional mayors and managers association to support the development of a downtown trolley line.

A very important related question is whether it makes sense to increase the board's size in order to achieve the diversity that we need and want. In my professional opinion, larger boards — up to a sensible maximum size — tend to make a more powerful contribution to out-of-the-box change, very simply because they bring more resources to the change game. Can a board be too large? I suppose so, but I've found that a far more common problem is boards that are too small, limiting the contribution that the boards can make to planning out-of-the-box change. This is to some extent the result of wrong-headed consultants traipsing around the country preaching board downsizing as a board development strategy. It doesn't take a rocket scientist to realize that the obvious costs of traveling down the slippery downsizing slope are pretty steep: less brainpower, knowledge, and expertise; reduced stature and visibility; less diversity in every sense; fewer connections in the wider world; less access to resources; to name some of the more important. And the benefits are not only few, but dubious: a board that's easier to manage (or, often, to control); that's less expensive to support; that's more cohesive (hardly a virtue when you think of identifying out-of-the-box issues). What's too big a board? There's no scientific answer, but I'd suggest that a twenty-one to thirty member board leaves room for considerable diversity without the risk of unwieldiness.

The majority of nonprofit boards have the power to fill their own vacancies, which gives them the maximum leverage in shaping their compositions, but many don't. The overwhelming majority of state, national, and international association boards, for example, are elected by association members, and the majority of public boards, such as school boards, city councils, and county commissions, are elected by the populations they represent. There are also many quasi-public boards, such as public transportation authorities and regional planning commissions, that are appointed by third parties, such as the mayor or chair of the county commission. And the size of the great majority of public and quasi-public boards is fixed by law, eliminating expansion as a tool to promote diversity. Even in these more constrained situations, however, there are steps that can be taken to strengthen the board as a human resource. For example, an association board's committee responsible for board development might develop a profile of the ideal board composition and make it available to the nominating committee, or even to the wider membership, to consider in coming up with, or voting for, candidates for vacant seats. A profile might also be shared with appointing authorities as a way to influence their selections.

Keep in mind that developing your board as a human resource isn't just a matter of influencing your board's composition. Education and training can be a powerful tool for preparing board members to participate in the Portfolio Process. For example, the orientation that your board's governance committee provides to every new board member can include a detailed description of your organization's Portfolio Process, including an explanation of the differences between mainstream and out-of-the-box planning, the rationale for going through the process in terms of outcomes and benefits, definitions of such key elements as values, vision, and out-of-the-box issues, and the nature of the board's involvement at key points in the process, such as the daylong retreat that kicks it off.

DEVELOPING YOUR BOARD'S GOVERNING ROLE AND WORK

Boards that have a pretty firm grasp of what governing is all about are far more likely to be productive contributors to the Portfolio Process than boards that are confused about what they're supposed to be doing in the boardroom. This is primarily because the confusion leaves board members unable to fit their change leadership role into a broader governing context. I'm sorry to say I've got some bad news to report in this regard. I've discovered in the process of interviewing thousands of board members that many, perhaps the majority, of nonprofit and public board members would be hard pressed to come up with a detailed definition of their board's governing role and major governing functions. When I've asked board members in telephone interviews what governing involves, in a nutshell, more often than not I've been told that what they do is policy making, a vague and erroneous answer that doesn't take us very far down the governing path. Policies are essentially rules to govern operations (such as human resource, financial management, and procurement policies), and very few are important enough to merit serious board consideration.

Keep in mind that once you've got a set of policies in place, updating them periodically isn't much of a challenge. So policy making really couldn't be more than a small part (I estimate an average of around 5 percent on an ongoing basis) of the work that your board does when it governs. What, then, is governing?

At the highest level, what boards do when they govern is answer three fundamental questions about your organization, working closely with the CEO and executive team: (1) the strategic question: What do we want our organization to be and do over the long run? (answered primarily by our vision statement and change initiatives); (2) Who are we now? (answered by our mission statement and annual operating plan and budget); and (3) How are we doing — operationally, programmatically, financially? (answered by regular monitoring and annual evaluation). If you drill down to a more nuts-and-bolts level, what you'll find is that when your board governs, what it essentially does is make a continuous stream of decisions and judgments about very concrete governing products and documents that flow along four main governing streams:

- **Board self-management**: decisions and judgments about such matters as developing your board's composition, setting board governing performance targets, monitoring board performance, and evaluating CEO performance.

- **Planning**: decisions about such long-range governing products as values and vision statements at the strategic end of the spectrum to adoption of the preeminent operational planning product, the annual budget, at the other end of the spectrum.

- **Performance monitoring**: judgments about organizational performance based on reviewing such governing documents as the quarterly financial report and monthly programmatic progress reports.

- **External relations**: decisions about the image our organization wants to convey to the wider world, the external stakeholders we should pay the most serious attention to, and the role board members should play in representing our organization externally.

The great majority of nonprofit and public organizations I've worked with have adopted a detailed description of the board's governing functions that is typically called the "governing mission" (the board's, not the organization's, mission). The CEOs of these organizations, wearing their Innovator-in-Chief hat, have made sure that their board's role in leading out-of-the-box change is explicitly included as an element of the governing mission. Let's take as an example the first few elements of the governing mission of a social service agency I worked with a few years ago, which I'll call PNI:

> *As the governing body of PNI, the Board of Directors is the steward and guardian of PNI values, vision, and mission; ensures that PNI is provided with the financial and other resources required to carry out its mission; sets clear, detailed strategic directions to guide PNI planning and program development;* ***ensures that PNI systematically invests in innovation aimed at capitalizing on growth opportunities and countering threats....***

Making systematic investment in innovation a board responsibility in your organization's governing mission lays the foundation for developing your board's detailed role in the Portfolio Process.

DEVELOPING YOUR BOARD'S GOVERNING STRUCTURE

When I first started working as a governance and change consultant in the nonprofit and public sectors, committee structure didn't make my top list of things I should worry about in helping organizations learn to govern more effectively. It didn't take me long, however, to learn that committees are one of the preeminent keys to governing effectiveness, along with developing the board as a human resource (especially building a diverse composition) and mapping out a clear, detailed governing role and set of well-defined governing functions. Most people would probably say that the most obvious benefit of board standing committees is more productive board meetings as a result of thorough committee preparation. But two less well-known functions of a well-designed committee structure are critical to your organization's accomplishing out-of-the-box change via the Portfolio Process. First, committees can serve as a vehicle for working out processes for meaningful board involvement in key governing areas, such as planning and performance oversight. Second, committees can serve as powerful change champions that take the lead in getting the board to make decisions.

Before going any further, note that I'm not talking about the functions and benefits of just any committees, but of a *well-designed* committee structure. What I mean is a set of standing committees that directly correspond to the streams of decisions and judgments making up your board's detailed governing work, adhering to the classic management maxim that form should always follow function. Accordingly, a well-designed committee structure for a nonprofit or public board will consist of:

- A **Governance or Board Operations Committee** accountable for coordinating the board's governing work, developing the board agenda, setting board performance targets and monitoring performance, and maintaining the board-CEO working relationship, including evaluating CEO performance.

- A **Planning Committee** accountable for working with the CEO in mapping out processes for involving board members in the planning cycle (all the way from values and vision to the annual operating plan and budget), coordinating board member involvement in planning, and recommending key planning products to the full board.

- A **Performance Monitoring Committee** accountable for working with the CEO in designing financial and programmatic performance reports that the board should regularly see, monitoring organizational performance, and reporting performance results to the full board.

- An **External Relations Committee** accountable for overseeing communication with key external stakeholders, coordinating board member involvement in external relations, and recommending board action on such governing products as an updated image statement, a set of external relations goals, and positions on key pieces of legislation in the hopper.

You can easily see that this contemporary committee structure (see Figure 3 on page 77) is the polar opposite of the old-fashioned silo committee structure that has caused so much organizational grief by inviting board members to put on their technical advisory or operational hats, hence promoting board micromanagement. A silo committee directly corresponds to either a particular program or service or to an administrative/operational function (rather than

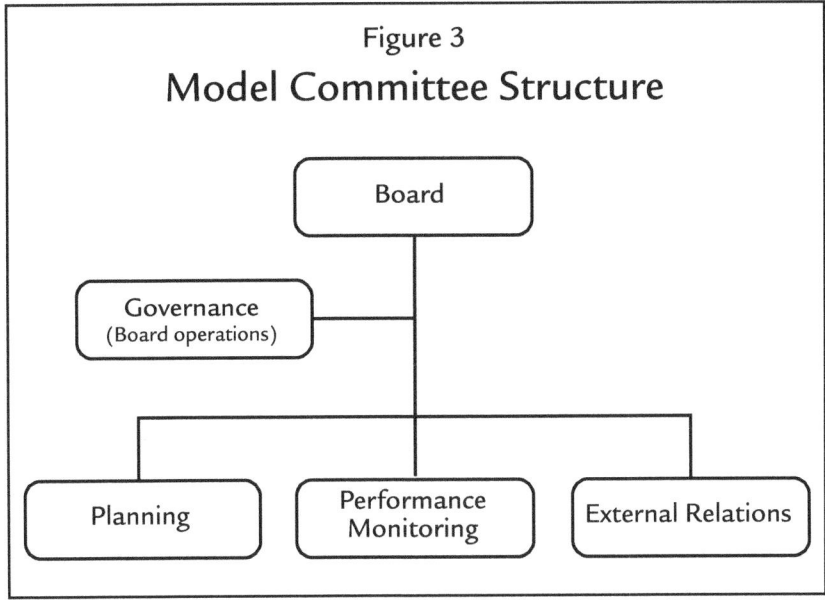

Figure 3
Model Committee Structure

to one of the broad governing streams I've been discussing). Here are some examples of silo committees that I've seen turn board members into micromanagers instead of governors: buildings and grounds (an operational function); personnel (an administrative function); education (a program or service); the annual conference (an operational function); rail operations (an operational function); curriculum and instruction (an administrative function); and residential services (a program). What a silo structure communicates to board members is "Come on in, get immersed in our programs and operations, help us run the shop." A board that's trapped in a silo structure is almost certainly not destined to lead out-of-the-box change!

Well-designed board committees, wearing the process design and change champion hats, would typically play the following roles in the Portfolio Process:

The Planning Committee

- Reaching agreement with the CEO on the detailed design of the process for engaging board members in your organization's application of the Portfolio Process; determining precisely what board members will be doing, when they will be doing it, and how they will be participating.

- Coordinating and overseeing board member participation in the Portfolio Process (for example, hosting a daylong strategic work session).

- Playing a hands-on role in shaping and recommending to the board key Portfolio products, such as an updated values statement, a set of issues to be addressed, and detailed change initiatives.

The Performance Monitoring Committee

- Reaching agreement with the CEO on the content, format, and frequency of performance reports that the committee will use to assess progress in carrying out the Portfolio Process.

- Monitoring implementation of the Portfolio Process.

- Recommending to the board action to deal with problems encountered in carrying out the Portfolio Process.

The External Relations Committee

- Reaching agreement with the CEO on the key elements of a communication process to keep the wider organization and external stakeholders briefed on progress in carrying out the Portfolio Process.

- Helping to make sure that key stakeholder representatives are involved, as appropriate, in the task forces that are created to fashion and implement the change initiatives in the CIP.

THE RETREAT AS A BOARD ENGAGEMENT TOOL

I've already touched on the usefulness of a board-CEO-executive team daylong planning session or retreat as a vehicle for engaging board members in a meaningful fashion early in the Portfolio Process, to accomplish such important out-of-the-box planning work as updating values and vision statements; identifying issues in the form of opportunities and challenges; and brainstorming possible change initiatives. A retreat has no peer in terms of creatively and proactively involving board members in the Portfolio Process if — and it's a big if — the retreat is well designed and executed. You shouldn't underestimate the risk involved in bringing your board members together in one room for a full day to deal with complex, high-stakes issues. I've lost count of the times I've been told horror stories of retreats that have fallen apart midstream because of inadequate facilitation, or alienated participants forced to participate in a poorly designed process, or that have ended up being a waste of time because of inadequate follow-through. My advice is: Do it right, or don't do it! Here are some practical tips for succeeding at the retreat game that I've learned over the course of facilitating hundreds of retreats:

- **Set aside enough time to do very important, highly complex planning work** — a full day at a minimum. Less than a day is a meeting, not a retreat.

- **Use an off-site location away from headquarters.** You don't need to foot the bill for a lavish resort, or even a nice hotel — the training room of a board member's company or even the comfortable social hall of a church might do — but you do need to get away from the shop as a means of fostering creativity and out-of-the-box thinking. Putting board members in their own board room is a tried-and-true way to squelch open-mindedness and keep people securely in the box.

- **Make sure the main meeting room is really spacious and comfortable** and, if possible, has windows. Being together for a full day dealing with high-stakes issues is taxing enough without adding claustrophobia to the mix. One of my design rules is to make sure everyone in the room can stand up and walk around freely at the same time without stumbling over each other.

- **Involve an ad hoc retreat design committee** headed by the board chair and consisting of several board members and the CEO to put together a detailed retreat design. If you've retained a professional facilitator to assist with the design, she will work with this committee. The detailed design, which will typically be in the range of five-to-seven pages, will include:

    The *outcomes the retreat is intended to produce* (for example, updated values and vision statements; the identification of issues facing the organization).

    The *structure of the retreat* (the setting; the participants; the breakout groups that will be employed).

    The *blow-by-blow agenda* (7:30 — continental breakfast; 8:00 — welcome; 8:10 — review of agenda; 8:20 — presentation by the planning committee on environmental conditions and trends; 8:45 — first round of breakout groups; etc.)

The *process for following through* (for example, the facilitator will write a follow-through report summarizing key points and recommending next steps; the planning committee will review the report; etc.)

- **Send the design to all invited participants at least a week before the retreat**, in the form of a memorandum from the members of the ad hoc retreat design committee and the facilitator.

- **Employ breakout groups led by board members to generate content** through a free-flowing brainstorming process (for example, an updated values statement; issues in the form of opportunities to grow). Make 100 percent sure that the board members leading breakout groups succeed in the leader role, primarily by providing detailed orientation and training. Board members who succeed publicly in the leader role will almost always become reliable champions for out-of-the-box change down the pike. A board member who fails publicly in leading a group, being embarrassed or even humiliated, won't likely be a supporter you can count on as the Portfolio Process moves forward.

- **Avoid trying to reach formal consensus or to make firm decisions.** Premature consensus and seat-of-the-pants decision making, especially if you take a patently gimmicky approach like voting with sticky dots, will almost certainly backfire, seriously damaging your retreat's credibility and leading to the inevitable unraveling of whatever premature decisions you made. A well-conceived follow-through process should be employed to make decisions subsequent to the retreat.

- Consider inviting participants outside of the inner circle of board and executive team members, as a way not only to infuse deliberations with new information and ideas, but also to build relationships with stakeholders whose support you might want down the road. A school district I worked with recently, for example, invited the mayor, planning commission chair, and community college vice president, among other outsiders. Avoiding formal voting ensures that expanding participation can't do any harm.

- And if you can afford to retain a **seasoned professional facilitator to help design the retreat and to facilitate the day**, by all means do so. It's a tried-and-true way to make sure you achieve everything you've set out to do — fully and on time.

FURTHER THOUGHTS ON THE BOARD-CEO PARTNERSHIP

By its very nature, the board-CEO working relationship is always fragile and capable of rapid erosion, primarily because of a highly combustible mix: strong-willed type As under tremendous pressure in a rapidly changing world that's continuously hurling complex issues in their direction. Developing a rock-solid board-CEO working relationship that can withstand the inevitable stresses and strains at the top isn't a piece of cake in any organization, but it's got to be a top priority concern if your organization intends to succeed in the change game. A dysfunctional board-CEO working relationship that's characterized by a high degree of tension and lack of cooperation and collaboration can jeopardize your organization's Portfolio Process if not repaired, for the simple reason that strong, top-down leadership is essential for securing staff and volunteer commitment to change initiatives and for overcoming organizational inertia and resistance. I've already discussed in detail four of the more important strategies for building a rock-solid board-CEO partnership: a CEO who enthusiastically embraces the Chief Board Developer role and plays it fully; a board that has a firm grasp of its governing role and functions; well-designed standing committees that serve as governing engines in accomplishing the board's detailed governing work; and involvement of the board in a proactive and meaningful fashion in the Portfolio Process, primarily via an intensive retreat early in the process.

Three other nuts-and-bolts steps I haven't discussed in detail yet have proved in practice to be highly effective partnership-building tools. First, assign to a particular board standing committee — typically executive, governance, or board operations — explicit responsibility for managing the board-CEO working relationship, including: updating the CEO position description as needed; annually reaching agreement with the CEO on her executive leadership goals and targets for the coming fiscal year; formally evaluating CEO performance at least annually, with the CEO present during the process; determining CEO compensation; and resolving board-CEO relationship issues that develop before they damage the board-CEO partnership.

Second, make sure that the process for board evaluation of CEO performance includes the negotiation of what I call "CEO-centric" performance goals and targets, not just organization-wide goals that are established through the annual operational planning/budget preparation process, and that these CEO-specific targets are used in evaluating performance. This is extraordinarily important because some of the most important issues that can jeopardize the board-CEO partnership relate to CEO performance specifically, rather than overall organizational performance. In fact, I've seen many more board-CEO relationships come to grief over CEO leadership issues than over organizational performance generally. Borrowed from real life, the following questions focus attention on CEO-specific performance targets. Should your public transportation authority's CEO play a major role in the external environment and, if so, approximately how much of his time should be devoted to precisely what external relations targets, such as rebuilding a frayed relationship with the board of county commissioners? Should your association's CEO play a major role in implementing a change initiative to consummate a merger with a sister association, and, if so, how much of your CEO's time should be devoted to carrying out this merger strategy? Should your CEO play a major role in helping the board become a more effective governing body, and, if so, what specific targets should she tackle, such as updating the board's committee structure?

Third, the board and CEO should reach explicit agreement on the rules that should govern board-CEO interaction. Will the CEO, for example, meet quarterly with every board member individually over breakfast or lunch? Will board members receive a weekly e-update from the CEO on major internal and external developments? What kind of early warning system should the CEO use to make sure board members aren't caught off guard by bad — or good — news? Is it clearly understood that only the board as a whole, speaking in one voice, can provide direction to the CEO, rather than individual board members?

BUILDING A SOLID BOARD CHAIR-CEO PARTNERSHIP

Before concluding this discussion of the board-CEO working relationship, I want to touch briefly on the board chair-CEO partnership, which is tremendously important because of the chair's highly visible and influential position in your organization's hierarchy. As you've no doubt learned, allowing this critical working relationship to erode would almost certainly seriously impede, and might even derail, the out-of-the-box change train. And, turning the coin over, if your board chair is a strong advocate and champion for change, your organization is much more likely to accomplish out-of-the-box change initiatives.

Your organization's CEO, wearing both the Innovator-in-Chief and Chief Board Developer hats, has to take the lead in developing and maintaining a rock-solid working relationship with his board chair, who, as a part-time, usually unpaid volunteer can't reasonably be expected to take the initiative in partnership building. The first step a board-savvy CEO will take is to reach agreement with his board chair on the basic, universally accepted division of labor, which will serve as an indispensable foundation for further relationship development:

> *The board chair is basically responsible for the work of the board, which includes: playing a major role in developing the board meeting agenda; chairing board meetings; and playing a key role, in her capacity as governance (or board operations) committee chair, in developing the board's governing capacity and maintaining the board-CEO partnership, including evaluation of CEO performance. The CEO, reporting directly to the full board, is accountable for all internal operations of the organization. The board chair and CEO both represent the organization externally, so they need to work out a mutually satisfactory division of labor on this front. One of the cardinal rules governing the board chair-CEO partnership is that the CEO reports only to, and takes direction only from, the board as a whole, never from the board chair or any individual board member.*

One of the key relationship-building objectives of a board-savvy CEO wearing the Innovator-in-Chief hat is to turn her board chair into an ardent champion for out-of-the-box change. I've seen three strategies work especially well in this regard. For one thing, the CEO can go out of her way to make sure her board chair becomes a true expert in the Portfolio Process so that the chair feels comfortable playing a leading role in the process. One of the board-savvier Innovators-in-Chief I've worked with, for example, made a point of bringing her board chair along to a two-day workshop I was presenting on taking command of change. I learned during one of the breaks that she'd also provided her chair with a couple of books on the subject, which they both read and discussed before the workshop.

The CEO can also make a special effort to ensure that her board chair plays a visible, influential, and ego-satisfying role in the Portfolio Process, feeling like a driver of the process rather than a bystander. To accomplish this, the CEO provides strong, hands-on support for her board chair in, for example:

- Chairing the ad hoc committee that develops the detailed design for the retreat kicking off the Portfolio Process.

- Keeping abreast of developments in the process via privy CEO briefings.

- Taking the lead in explaining the Portfolio Process to internal and external stakeholders, including the media.

- Presenting charges in person to task forces that are formed to develop change initiatives.

- And sitting in on planning committee meetings at which task forces are presenting preliminary and finished change initiatives.

And the CEO can, within reason, take her board chair's professional interests into account in engineering opportunities for her chair's involvement in the Portfolio Process. For example, an association CEO I worked with, knowing that the chair of her association board was passionately interested in growing the association internationally, made sure that her chair was invited to sit in on key meetings of the task force that'd been charged to fashion a strategic initiative aimed at international growth. This CEO went even further, encouraging her chair to participate actively in the discussion, rather than merely sitting on the sidelines as a silent authority figure. Of course, the CEO counseled her chair on how to participate without pulling rank and putting a damper on discussion.

Postscript

UP CLOSE AND PERSONAL

A POTENT PERSONAL GROWTH TOOL: MY PERSONAL EXPERIENCE

I'm a passionate believer in the portfolio process that you've been reading about in this book, not because it's especially theoretically fascinating, but because it works, making a tremendous positive difference in a world that's rapidly changing, always challenging, and quite often discombobulating. It's the preeminent key to your organization's long-term stability and growth. But my passion is also really close-up and personal. The fact is, if it weren't for the Change Investment Portfolio Process I've described in this book, I wouldn't be enjoying a career that fits my intellectual and emotional makeup so closely, capitalizes so fully on my skills, and provides me with such deep satisfaction. Let me tell you something about my own growth journey and why over the years I've become such a fervent adherent to the portfolio approach to leading change in my life.

I guess I'm what you'd call a late bloomer in the personal out-of-the-box change game. I loved teaching ancient history and English at Tafari Makonnen Secondary School in Addis Ababa, Ethiopia, for three years after earning my BA at the University of Illinois. Teaching felt like a close fit at the time with both my skills and emotional makeup, providing me with really deep satisfaction. So I'm not really sure why, when I returned to the United States, I turned down a handsome fellowship in a master of arts in teaching program and, instead, went to business school. Looking back, it was probably a classic case of marching to a tune being played by people around me rather than setting my own course. I do recall thinking about the relatively greater prestige and earning power of management versus teaching and worrying that I'd sorely disappoint my mother if I ended up in a high school classroom. Anyway, I spent the next fifteen years working in five different senior management positions in the nonprofit and public sectors, quite capably, I think, but certainly without much passion or joy. My ever richer personal life, however — marriage, children, buying my first home in a very attractive suburb of Cleveland, Ohio, socializing with other parents on our street of young families — did dull the pain considerably for quite some time.

But by the mid-1980s, the feeling of emptiness, professionally speaking, had grown so acute that a happy family life wasn't enough to keep the pain at bay, and I found myself increasingly caught up in unhealthy coping behavior, compulsively exercising in the wee hours of the morning and drinking too many glasses of wine in the evening, both of which were taking a toll on my marriage. I was beginning to feel like a nervous breakdown was in the offing when I finally decided to confront the pain head-on: trying to figure out what was going on and deciding what to do about it, rather than continuing to anesthetize myself and making life miserable for my wife and kids. So, in desperation, I did my first serious visioning on the professional front. Spending a week alone, I thought long and hard about the kind of professional life that would fit both my abilities and my emotional needs, painting a picture that looks pretty much like my professional life now: returning to my first professional love by doing work that is essentially educational, through consulting, speaking, and writing; being my own boss; setting my own schedule; working out of my home rather than commuting to the office. I realized that working with nonprofit and public organizations at the board- and CEO-level made good sense, in light of my knowledge and expertise at this point in my life, but that I couldn't be happy as an executive any longer. I clearly had to teach, but it didn't have to be in the classroom.

Once I'd fleshed out my professional vision, it wasn't that hard to put together a set of change initiatives for my new personal Change Investment Portfolio, aimed at getting my new business venture underway: negotiating a phase-out contract with my then-employer; deciding what customers my new business would sell to; refining my products and services; setting up my first office, in an apartment on the third floor of our home; developing a promotional brochure, etc. And, to be honest, it certainly helped that my wife, a nonprofit executive, could pay the mortgage while I was getting started. But none of this essentially technical business start-up work would mean anything unless I figured out how to surmount a huge barrier — a true out-of-the-box issue standing in the way of translating my new vision into reality: my tremendous fear of public speaking. In light of the very complex emotional factors that made me so extremely self-conscious at the podium, becoming an effective public speaker was easily the most challenging issue I had to address in my Change Portfolio.

The change initiative I put together to transform me into a competent public speaker involved working with a psychotherapist to understand why I felt so much performance anxiety, retaining a speech coach to teach me tricks of the trade, learning to use PowerPoint not only as a visual aid but also as a tool to relax me, and employing just plain old-fashioned discipline: accepting speaking engagements no matter how nervous I felt and eventually realizing that I not only wouldn't keel over at the podium, I could actually acquit myself well and even have fun. By the way, I still feel a dollop of performance anxiety whenever I approach the podium, but over the years I've learned that I can put it to good use in communicating with audiences, keeping me on my toes and preventing the kind of been there, done that feel from creeping into my performances and boring my audiences to death.

I want you to know that since my original foray into formal change portfolio planning and management, I've made ever more conscious and systematic use of the process professionally, not only to grow my business, but also to develop my professional skills. At any given time, my out-of-the-box portfolio includes a small number of change initiatives — never more than three or four at a time — related to both business targets (for example, writing a book dramatically different from any I'd done before, *The Blind Visionary*, and developing a new speaking business based on the book), and expanding my own capability (for example, enrolling in an acting class to bring more emotional honesty and depth to my presentations). I manage my change portfolio completely separately from my normal, day-to-day work, never mixing the two up. And over the years since making the major career change that got me on the right track after years of doing unsatisfying administrative work, I've relied on my evolving vision to guide my choice of issues to add to my Change Investment Portfolio.

I certainly don't mean that I update a formal vision statement every year; as I explain below, that's not the way individuals, unlike organizations, do visioning. But I pay close attention to the signals — from both inside and outside — that can lead me to repaint or fill in some part of my personal canvas, leading to the identification of new opportunities and challenges and the development of new change initiatives. To take a recent pretty dramatic example, over the past year I've reunited with two former Ethiopian students of mine, who lived with me and my housemates in Addis Ababa, over forty years ago. I'd completely lost track of Tesfagiorgis and Tariku over the years since returning to the United States from Ethiopia and assumed they'd been killed under the extremely violent regime after Emperor Haile Selassie's overthrow. Thanks to the wonders of the web, we've found each other, and I've learned enough of their personal histories since we said good-bye in Addis in 1967, including their imprisonment for two years and near-execution, to know that it's a miracle they're alive and that we've reunited, and that they have a wonderful story to tell. This is clearly an opportunity for me to write another very different book, expanding my vision of what's possible as a writer, and as I finish the manuscript of the book you are now reading, I'm also — within my Change Investment Portfolio — translating this opportunity and expanded vision into a concrete change initiative: outlining the new book and getting it written.

SOME PRACTICAL GUIDANCE

Recognizing the tremendous difference that the portfolio approach to personal change has made in my life and the lives of many of my friends and colleagues, I felt that I had no choice but to bring *Leading Out-of-the-Box Change* to a close with some practical thoughts on how to go about making use of a variation on the Portfolio Process to build a richer, more satisfying personal and professional life for yourself. Don't think for a minute that I'm suggesting that you can simply plunk down the organizational version of the portfolio approach carte blanche, with all of its formal planning and management bells and whistles, in your own life. What I am saying is that you can make use of the broad logic and methodology of the approach in growing your life, but you'll find that the personal application (which I like to think of as the "Personal Change Portfolio Process") differs in important ways from the organizational. Keep the following points in mind as you lead change in your own life:

- Your aim in applying the personal portfolio process is to build a life, personally and professionally, that is true to who you fundamentally are, at a deep level — in terms of your evolving vision of the right life for you — one that meets your emotional needs and reflects your core values — and that will provide you with a sense of deep meaning and satisfaction.

- Don't think of your personal application of the portfolio approach as a formal planning cycle that you put yourself through year after year, updating a formal vision statement, identifying issues, fashioning and implementing change initiatives, etc. Rather, think of it as a powerful tool that you keep in your personal growth kit, available to you whenever you need to make use of it.

- Vision — the picture of the personal and professional life you aspire to lead — is even more critical in the personal context than the organizational, but on the personal front, we're talking about a much less formal, far more fluid visioning process — more of an unfolding drama of learning and discovery than a formal step in a planning process.

- The psychological and emotional dimension looms much larger in the personal application than in the organizational, making personal out-of-the-box change more complex and problematic than organizational, particularly because of the powerful role that deep-seated, unconscious emotions can play. The unconscious dimension also makes self-deception a clear and present danger at all times.

- You can expect to find the personal application much more viscerally fearsome than the organizational because the stakes involved are so close to home. (It's your potential failure, your potential embarrassment, or your potential humiliation that's at stake, not your organization's.)

- And then there's the always-mysterious spiritual dimension, which many people, including myself, have found a source of courage in facing fearsome change. In my book, *The Blind Visionary*, my coauthor, Virginia Jacko, testifies that her Catholic faith has been extremely important in mustering the courage to move forward on a new career path after losing her eyesight. This is not to say that spirituality and religion are synonymous; they can be, but often aren't.

A CAVEAT ABOUT GOAL SETTING

Setting targets, mapping out plans for hitting them, and rigorously managing implementation are very familiar, satisfying territory for ambitious, high-achieving, often type-A human beings. (This probably describes the great majority of my readers.) Being really good at this kind of operational planning and management is extraordinarily important to your professional success in the short run in handling in-the-box operational issues, and it's the engine that drives day-to-day organizational performance. It's also critical in fashioning plans to implement change initiatives in your out-of-the-box change portfolio. Without question it's high priority stuff; you're likely to lose your job if you miss too many deadlines, or screw up implementation of a critical change initiative. It's also an essential tool for managing your personal life. After all, you really do need to do careful personal budgeting and financial management, including saving for retirement and the kids' college, and you want to make sure that you and your significant other or spouse set aside enough personal time to keep your relationship healthy.

But be careful that you don't click into a goal-setting mindset prematurely when you're venturing into the realm of personal out-of-the-box change. The very concreteness and familiarity of traditional goal setting make it a kind of siren song that, if you're not vigilant, can lure you away much too soon from the far less concrete, much more emotional, often quite frightening experience-driven process of expanding your vision and capitalizing on opportunities to translate your expanded vision into change initiatives. I'm sure you've met people — I certainly have come across many — who have very capably planned and managed themselves into careers that don't begin to tap their tremendous potential and leave them empty and dissatisfied, and into personal lives that are lonely or arid. Be forewarned!

SOME CLOSING THOUGHTS ON PERSONAL VISIONING

I've never come across a person who regularly updated a formal, personal vision statement, and I can't imagine formally updating my own vision on a regular basis as part of some sort of personal strategic planning process. Instead, in real life, so far as I can tell, a person's vision, rather than being formally planned according to some kind of schedule, unfolds over the course of a person's life, through a largely informal process of learning from — being educated by — experience. Visioning is a process that takes place at the intersection of your objective experience and your mind, in terms both of conscious reasoning and the emotional realm of feeling. In a nutshell, as the years pass, our emotional and intellectual responses to certain experiences lead to expansion and revision of our personal and professional visions, through a process that is so informal and often subtle that we don't even recognize how our vision has evolved until long after the fact. Sometimes the experiences are dramatic and abrupt, easily commanding our attention and eliciting a strong emotional response: for example, you lose your job or your spouse initiates divorce proceedings. Sometimes the experiences last for an extended period, educating us more slowly: for example, as I discuss in the opening section of this Postscript, the growing sense of emptiness and dissatisfaction connected to my working in executive management positions for fifteen years.

To take some real-life examples, at the more dramatic end of the spectrum is the experience of a close friend and former teacher of mine, then in his mid-seventies — a distinguished professor of management, a Jew who had for years adamantly resisted any involvement in the religious aspect of Judaism. One afternoon he was walking by a storefront Orthodox synagogue, when he heard loud singing. As he told me later, he felt a powerful emotional jolt out of the blue. Not understanding what was going on, he stopped and looked in the open door to see dark-suited and hatted men in a circle singing and dancing. Tears streaming down his face, he stood there for a few minutes, until the circle opened up and he was motioned in. He danced for a few minutes, feeling, as he told me, that he'd in some deep sense come home. For the rest of his life, "Grundy," as I knew him, was an observant Orthodox Jew, attending synagogue faithfully and observing dietary restrictions for the first time in his adult life.

Another example of being dramatically educated by experience involves a woman I know well — a highly creative graphic artist — who'd taken a job heading the graphics department of a consulting firm, lured by the salary and other perks. You might say this was an example of poor visioning, in contrast to Grundy's discovery of a part of himself he'd kept at bay for years. Fired after less than a year on the job, Karen — humiliated and devastated (she'd never failed in any major way professionally before this) — curled up in a ball to lick her wounds, bitter at what she saw as brutal mistreatment. But as she reflected on her experience, she eventually realized that her true professional vision — her fundamental source of satisfaction and fulfillment — was to create directly, as a graphic artist, not to manage a shop of artists. She actually came to believe that she'd sabotaged herself in her corporate job, unconsciously asking to be fired, as a result of straying from her true vision, even though she wasn't consciously aware of it at the time.

At the less dramatic end of the change spectrum is a vision that unfolds over quite some time and feels like discovering some true side of yourself — of what you are meant to be and do. I have always loved the true story of a teenager who the summer he turned fourteen worked in his dad's bakery in the small Illinois town where he'd grown up. With the money he saved that summer from his $36-a-week paycheck, he bought a cheap record player and, without thinking much about it, joined the classical division of the Columbia record club. Every month a new record showed up in the mail, and over a couple of years he was introduced to the mainstream classical repertory: Beethoven, Tchaikovsky, Brahms, Mendelssohn, Mozart — the whole crew. As he observed years later, "Listening to those records taught me that the good life I aspired to live had to include easy access to classical music, not just on record but even more important, in live performance." He discovered, rather than planned, an important part of his vision, and, by the way, he acted on that vision as the years passed, primarily by choosing to live and work in cities with reasonably strong, if not always top-tier, symphony orchestras that played a full season.

In his remarkable book, *The Art of Judgment,* Sir Geoffrey Vickers tells the true story of a professor who'd never thought of teaching abroad until he was invited to apply for a position at a Canadian university. He didn't apply, but from that point on his professional vision now encompassed the possibility of teaching in another country, and eventually he did end up relocating to Canada to teach. This is another facet of personal visioning: widening the lens through which we see opportunities for change.

Can you get better at visioning? In my opinion, you definitely can, but it won't be by sharpening your technical planning skills. Rather, the preeminent key to visioning is paying close attention to the emotional signals that are elicited by events you experience in your life journey, whether positive or negative, and asking yourself what the feelings mean, whether they might call for moving in new directions in your life. And you've always got to be on guard against blocking out uncomfortable feelings, such as fear and anxiety, or, worse, using alcohol or some other anesthetic to blunt the pain.

ABOUT THE AUTHOR

Doug Eadie is the founder and president of Doug Eadie & Company, a firm that specializes in helping nonprofit and public organizations develop board and CEO leadership capacity, build solid board-CEO partnerships, and take command of strategic change. During the past twenty-five years, Doug has worked with more than 500 public and nonprofit organizations.

He is the author of eighteen books on nonprofit leadership in addition to *Leading Out-of-the-Box Change*, including *The Blind Visionary*, *Building a Rock-Solid Partnership With Your Board*, and *Meeting the Governing Challenge*. Before founding his consulting practice, Doug served as a Peace Corps Volunteer for three years in Addis Ababa, Ethiopia, and held several senior positions in the public and nonprofit sectors. He is a Phi Beta Kappa graduate of the University of Illinois at Urbana and received his master of science in management degree from the Weatherhead School at Case Western Reserve University.

Visit www.DougEadie.com to find out more about Doug Eadie & Company's custom-tailored consulting services, retreats, workshops, and webinar programs.

Milton Keynes UK
Ingram Content Group UK Ltd.
UKHW011346250224
438379UK00001B/184